Graham Sutherland, 'Creation', 1950, the origins of these writings.

GEOFFREY
JELLICOE

The Studies of a Landscape Designer over 80 Years

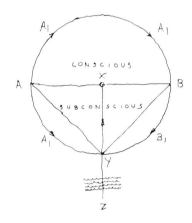

VOLUME I

Soundings
An Italian Study 1923-1925
Baroque Gardens of Austria

GARDEN · ART · PRESS

Printed on Consort Royal Satin from Donside Mills, Aberdeen

Published by Garden Art Press
a division of Antique Collectors' Club Ltd.
Printed in England by the Antique Collectors' Club Ltd., Woodbridge, Suffolk IP12 1DS

THE STUDIES OF A
LANDSCAPE DESIGNER

This four-volume collection of writings comprehend some seventy years of the practice, experience and philosophy of landscape design. They describe how the concept of an active subconscious is emerging to help organise and give meaning to the making of the modern environment. The Greek philosopher Heraclitus (500 B.C.) wrote: 'The unconscious harmonises the conscious'.

The Writings are in four volumes:

Volume I: *Soundings,* being an introductory personal tour through conscious and subconscious time

An Italian Study, being a critical study of the original drawings in *Italian Gardens of the Renaissance*

Baroque Gardens of Austria

Volume II: *Gardens and Design* and *Gardens of Europe;* pre-war studies, critical and creative

Volume III: *Studies in Landscape Design,* where the concept of the subconscious emerges

Volume IV: *The Guelph Lectures on Landscape Design, Instinct and Mind* and *Jung and the Art of Landscape*

CONTENTS

INTRODUCTION
TO
VOLUME I

Soundings, a saga of seven decades of practice, is intended to convey to the reader exactly the same feelings towards the subconscious in creative design that I myself have experienced, and so prepare him or her more fully for the sequences that lead to the climax in *Jung and the Art of Landscape* (Volume IV).

There follows *An Italian Study,* a critical reappraisal and analysis of *Italian Gardens of the Renaissance,* which began it all in 1925; and *Baroque Gardens of Austria* which especially opened the window on the relationship of music and architecture and landscape.

SOUNDINGS

CONTENTS

Eileen Agar: 'The Autobiography of an Embryo', 1933-4
The artist described this large painting as a 'celebration of life' which suggests the [subconscious]
memories of nature and primitive art that are born with a human child. The four separate pictures
make a sequence to be read from left to right, in which the repeated circles that form each design
resemble cells dividing into complicated patterns. At the left these are random, but at the right they
finally make a shape like the beginning of a human face. Small rectangles, like a collage of postcards,
show primitive sculptures, which are also here imagined to be embedded in the unconscious mind
of the baby before birth. The Tate Gallery Illustrated Biennial Report 1986-88

FOREWORD

This brief voyage through seven decades of practice and experience is intended to give meaning to the four volumes that will comprise the *Collected Writings*. Beginning with the 1925 study of Italian classical form, you are guided by degrees into the strange unexplored and inspiring regions of the subconscious mind, whose creative power in landscape design has yet to be recognised.

It is said that a child's natural instincts at birth are already fully developed, but that it cannot communicate. During the first decade of a happy childhood my own instincts expanded and responded to natural landscapes, especially to fresh and sea water, sand, hide-and-seek forests, climbable trees and games including hunting humans, but not animals. In the second decade I was curious about houses of all kinds, the Pre-Raphaelites and William Morris, cathedrals and ruined castles, the Versailles of Louis Seize and Marie Antoinette, mazes, chess, cricket and football. I clearly had an interest in building and in the arts generally (but very little in gardens and landscape). I entered the Architectural Association's school of architecture on or about the first of January 1919. Flirtation with the arts was over, the professional soundings of one of the world's great mysteries was to begin.

DECADE 1920-1930:
CLASSICAL AND ROMANTIC

I

At the Architectural Association you were, of course, first taught to draw. You experienced the pleasures of the drawing board, the T-square, the set square, cartridge and tracing paper, and how to slice off enough of the latter without losing the lot. You were taught about the right pencil and how to rub down Indian ink; and how to rub out. These were the tools of the trade for the soundings that were soon to begin.

The AA school at that time was very different in its philosophy from what it is today, arguably the most avant-garde in the world. It was recovering slowly after the First World War, with teaching staff relying on the pre-war tried formulae of classicism. You soaked in Rome and the Renaissance in Italy, France and England. The method of learning in principle was through (a) the measured drawing either from paper or reality; (b) the creation of your own pictorial Roman composition that usually included a column, parts of a portico and a trophy of arms (an exercise that can be traced back to eighteenth century England); and (c) the study and appreciation of the current grand Roman-inspired compositions of the Ecole des Beaux-Arts in Paris. You then designed the programme you were given in the style of your choice. The isolation from the great movements through Europe — of Le Corbusier, whom I was to appreciate in the next decade, of Picasso in the fourth decade, Carl Jung in the sixth, and Einstein in the seventh — was complete. The academic method was soon to be outmoded, but behind it were certain qualities and values that western civilisation maybe cannot afford to lose. I quote from my final lecture to the students of Guelph University, Ontario, delivered in the seventh decade:

> If we liken our present civilisation to a ship voyaging in unchartered, dangerous seas, with no knowledge of where we are going and indeed why — then its structure is critical. Our present ship is built of the tested materials of classicism and these we should be unwise to discard until we are certain that those of a new structure are stronger and more appropriate. But this does not apply to the contents of the ship, and as furnishings we can dredge things out of the deep that we never even dreamed existed.

So let us examine the method of teaching at close quarters.

As an exercise in the second year I was asked to draw the Roman Temple of Castor and Pollux to an enlarged scale from book illustrations of the whole and the parts. I was only a fair architectural draughtsman but as the great portico evolved on the paper before me and came to life with the shadows, I was overwhelmed with its majesty and the humanity of its details; this indeed was beauty. In the same year I measured up the portico of the church of St. Mary le Bow, Cheapside, and in the following year spent my vacation in sketching further aspects of Christopher Wren's London — sketches with a technique too woolly for an architect, who must be precise, and which were to lie fallow for sixty years.

As late as the third year I recall working on a project with a plate of a particularly enticing Ecole-des-Beaux Arts composition on my drawing board

Capital of the temple of Castor and Pollux, Rome, from Desgodetz's Architectural Antiquities

PORTION
OF
DOOR

ST.MARY-
LE-BOW

CHEAPSIDE

7/8/21

Door at St. Mary-le-Bow, Cheapside, drawing from 1921 sketchbook

beside me, and a wealth of Louis Seize decoration illustrations scattered around. An English academic example to students at that time, also, was the pre-war Ritz Hotel in Piccadilly by Mewes and Davis, with its fine anglo-classical plan and accomplished French decor.

The outstanding contemporary book was Geoffrey Scott's *Architecture of Humanism,* difficult to read but revolutionary to students smothered in tired neo-classicism. The argument, ably conducted through a series of 'fallacies', is directed towards a return to classical purity. It accepts no challenge to its thesis, ignores romantic architecture, gardens and landscapes, and abhors reinforced concrete as destructive to the acknowledged canons of proportion. What we students liked was its integrity and search for truth.

For me personally, the *Discourses* of Joshua Reynolds were, and still are, a milestone in aesthetic judgement, containing the immortal statement (more vital than ever today in this age of community) that an artist should never lower himself to the proletariat, but if possible he should raise the proletariat to his own standards. The title of the intriguing *Studies in Architecture* by Ralph Adams Cram provided the title thirty years later of *Studies in Landscape Design.*

As with the sister arts, the Rome Prize in architecture has generally been accepted as the blue ribbon of the student world. The finalists are selected from

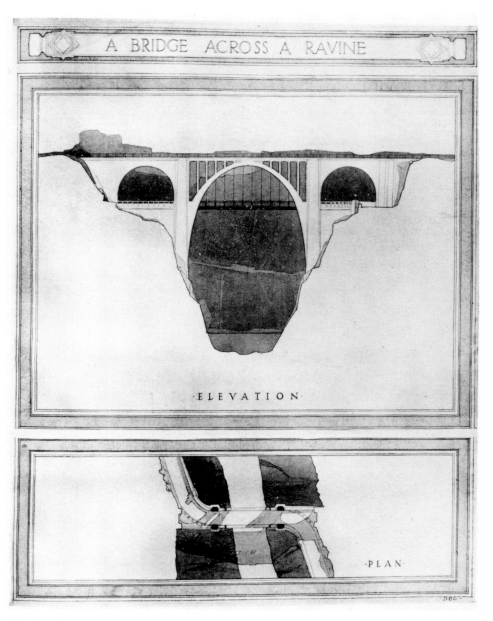

J.C. Shepherd's design for a bridge across a ravine, entered for the Rome Prize, 1923. (Courtesy The Architectural Association)

a first-round competition. In 1923 four were entered by the Architectural Association. The programme was for a bridge across a rocky ravine. Three of us were accepted and the one to fail, J C Shepherd was by common staff and student consent the most talented. My own design was based on Roman scenes by Piranesi, whose fantastic prints could at that time be bought for ten shillings [50p] in the Charing Cross Road. Shepherd's design was a graceful reinforced concrete structure inspired by the Swiss engineer Robert Maillart. The forward-looking principal of the school, Howard Robertson, stoutly defended the failed design and the incident proved a turning point in the philosophical history of the AA.

Watercolour of Rome, by Jock Shepherd, c.1925

II

The four and a half years of education in architecture were composed equally of highly charged take-in and give-out experience. The batteries had to be continuously recharged. Although the aesthetic in-take at this time was limited to historic styles, the student undoubtedly emerged with a developed sense of composition that was abstract and basic. In retrospect it is my view that, with obvious exceptions, the critical faculties of a student in his final years are at their most acute; but they have been overworked. A sabbatical year of in-take only, in many cases made possible by grant or scholarship, seems essential as a prelude to practice and the struggle for existence.

On completion of the course at the AA Jock Shepherd and I joined forces in the summer of 1923 to travel as freelances on a one year tour of Europe. We both felt the need of a realistic grounding in the classics before tackling the modern world which we knew to be upon us. Some nine months would be spent in classical Italy and thereafter we should travel north to Scandinavia, experiencing only modern architecture on the way. Since we considered it advisable to anchor ourselves to one specific subject to study in detail, my own thoughts ranged from cathedrals to theatres. In the event we settled, almost by chance, on gardens, formal gardens, as a subject little known in this country. In October we visited our first garden, the Villa Dona dalle Rose, Valzanzibio, in the Euganian hills of northern Italy. I measured the gardens by pacing, and that night in the hotel drew out the plan. The effect was staggering. The drawing that slowly emerged revealed that the substance of the beauty of a garden could be transmitted to paper. That night we knew we were on a remarkable voyage of discovery, ending in a serious contribution to knowledge. *Italian Gardens of the Renaissance* was published two years later and, whether I was suitable or not, my career began as a landscape architect. (I sometimes ruminate as to whether I should have had an equally agreeable career as a theatre designer, for which I seem to have had the greater urge.)

It must be made known to the reader that at this period of in-take we were puritanical followers of Geoffrey Scott. We took no interest in English romantic landscape, scarcely knew the difference between a buttercup and a daisy, and considered Baroque too decadent for inclusion (in later editions we mellowed towards Baroque, including the lovely Isola Bella on Lake Maggiore, possibly the most romantic folly in the classical world. We also excluded the Villa d'Este at Tivoli on the score of vulgarity of detail, but this decision was rescinded later and the plan copied from a faulty earlier drawing).

Italian gardens are described elsewhere but, for contrasting reasons, two are memorable for breaking the tradition that the classical garden is solely an extension of the house and subservient to it — or, as Alberti has written, a podium to it. The climax of Renaissance garden design is the Villa Lante, Bagnaia, by Vignola and here, perhaps for the first time in western classical history, the *idea* of the landcape predominates over that of the house. Lante, however, was still bound to the academic collective tradition of the geometric symmetry that expresses the human body. The Villa Gamberaia, Settignano,

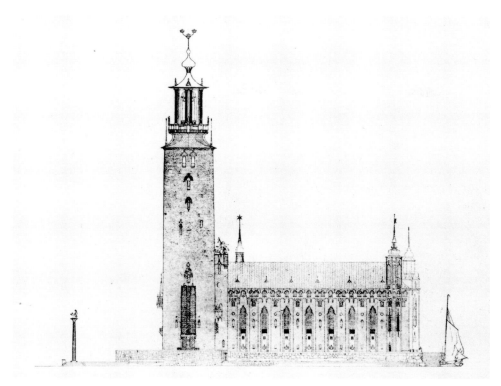

Stockholm City Hall by Ragnas Ostberg

near Florence — made later in the period known as Mannerism — goes further in breaking completely from the collective concept of symmetrical geometry of house and garden. The significance of this to the modern world is discussed during the next decade; for me it remains the keystone in all future thoughts on the individual garden.

With one foot now planted on the firm ground of acknowledged values we started north to take soundings of the modern world. We were entertained in Zurich by the architect Werner Moser who advised us to reach Scandinavia via Holland rather than France, and especially see the work of Hendrick Berlage. We crossed to Stockholm where Ragnas Ostberg took us round his newly built city hall. We returned to England via Norway. I believe that Jock Shepherd was permanently influenced by the transitional romanticism we experienced in this tour to the north and that it was this that inspired the competition design for the Shakespeare Memorial Theatre at Stratford-upon-Avon that he won later with Elizabeth Scott. Like myself, he remained only on the fringe of the modernism of the next decade.

III

So we came home and, after some nominal office experience, set up in practice on the strength of a house or two of friends and relations. At first we could only think geometrically. In Italy all gardens had seemed static, but not so in England where I was astonished, for instance, at how quick off the mark are runner beans. But we were soon acclimatised, particularly admiring the combination of Lutyens and Jekyll and the organic domestic architecture of

Frank Lloyd Wright. By absorbing the beauties of the English countryside, and urged on by the publishers, we felt after two or three years confident enough to follow *Italian Gardens of the Renaissance* with a general theoretic study later entitled *Gardens and Design.*

Until the mid-1920s my mentor was the brilliant Jock Shepherd, but with the great in-take over and properly digested, I began on my own tentatively to explore the meaning of art and environment — to begin the soundings that have never ceased. My first assaults on modern art were intellectual: I chose to interview five well known English sculptors for an article in the AA Journal. These were Eric Gill, Frank Dobson, Elizabeth Muntz, Eric Kennington and Henry Moore — sculptors I felt to be on the threshold of a world far removed from the academic, and one which I did not understand.

For me the five sculptors stood like sentinels at the entrance to this unknown world. Frank Dobson in Hammersmith Mall would stroke his (to me) oddly distorted figure and declare which part had come alive and which by gentle chiselling still had to become so. A weekend with Eric Kennington in his country home near Reading revealed how he would break off a conversation when the creative spirit suddenly urged, disappear to his studio and return as though he had never left; his subconscious was all-powerful. Elizabeth Muntz in Nottingham explained the use of latitudinal line in a sculptor's drawing to delineate form; and Eric Gill dispensed tea and wisdom in his remote home above High Wycombe.

Unlike most artists, Henry Moore in his Hampstead studio was eminently loquacious. He discoursed on his theory of art to an eager questioner for nearly three hours. I have no record of this, but the essence is contained in a published statement made by him a few years later:

> *Vitality and power of expression.* For me a work must first have a vitality of its own. I do not mean a reflection of the vitality of life, of movement, physical action, frisking, dancing figures and so on, but that a work can have in it a pent-up energy, an intense life of its own, independent of the object it may represent. When a work has this powerful vitality we do not connect the word Beauty with it.
>
> Beauty, in the later Greek or Renaissance sense, is not the aim of my sculpture.
>
> Between beauty of expression and power of expression there is a difference of function. The first aims at pleasing the senses, the second has a spiritual vitality which for me is more moving and goes deeper than the senses.
>
> Because a work does not aim at reproducing natural appearance it is not, therefore, an escape from life — but may be a penetration into reality, not a sedative or drug, not just the exercise of good taste, the provision of pleasant shapes and colours in a pleasing combination, not a decoration to life, but an expression of the significance of life, a stimulation to a greater effort in living.

I came away deeply impressed by Moore's generous personality and his confidence in his extraordinary interpretation of art. I remained, however, repelled by his sculpture.

Henry Moore, 'Maternity', 1924

Henri Gaudier-Brzeska, 'Red Stone Dancer', 1914

Shortly after this I was in a friend's house discussing a fee for a minor professional report. I hardly liked to propose cash and on the mantel-piece was a very small bronze abstract figure with the kind of shape I had so disliked in the Moore sculpture. I was suddenly and illogically drawn towards it, asked for it in payment, and was given it by a client who was indifferent to it. I took it home and showed it to Jock Shepherd and other architects, all of whom smiled it off. Under duress I had to sell it later to the Leicester Galleries for seven guineas [£7.35], the fee I should have charged. It was, in fact, the work of the great sculptor Henri Gaudier-Brzeska whom Moore acknowledged as his predecessor and of whom I had never heard.

Something had passed between myself and the sculpture, or rather the spirit of the artist within the sculpture. This something was beyond all previous experience and gave me my first assurance that I could make my own private and personal contacts through the subconscious. In the event it was twenty years before any further such amorphous contact was made, when I was suddenly to recognise Moore as the greatest sculptor of the century. So, too, was it with modern painting, which meant even less. The next decade was to be devoted solely to the understanding of contemporary architecture, with some thoughts on modern landscape design lightly thrown in.

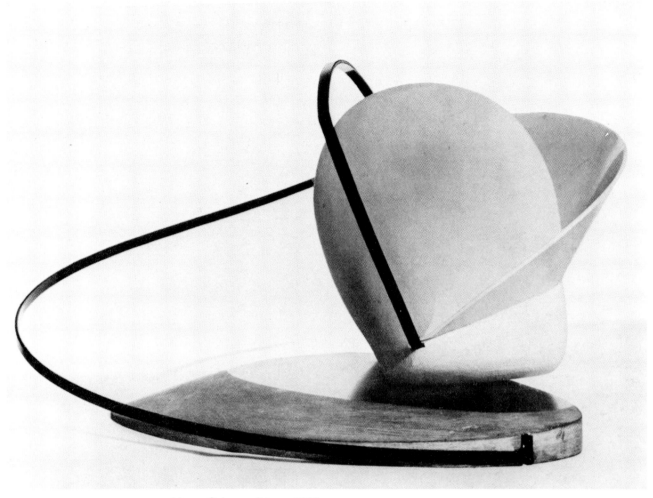

Naum Gabo, sculpture, 1929

DECADE 1930-1940:
MODERN ARCHITECTURE

I

A further six-month tour proved to be symbolic of my duality of thought, historical and modern, throughout the decade. On the one hand I was deeply impressed by Greek philosophy which I now experienced either in the shady gardens of the British School in Athens or in the sight of a Doric temple that seemed like an abode of the gods come to rest upon our unruly planet. On the other hand, and as a sequel to *Italian Gardens of the Renaissance,* I collected the material for, and later published, *Baroque Gardens of Austria* — a robust Roman concept far removed from spiritual Greece.

The duality was to be reflected in my opposing soundings in design. One half of my time was spent as a master in the third year studios of the Architectural Association, and the other half in building up a solo practice through any chance commission that might float by and be caught. The one introduced me through questioning students to the concept of modern architecture, and the other to the creation of a highly accomplished neo-classical practice in garden design arising from *Italian Gardens of the Renaissance.* During the decade I practised both philosophies equally, keeping them apart.

II

The publication of *Circle* of 1937 is the most complete credo of the modern English movement of the 1930s. Although not specifically mentioned, the acknowledgement to Greek spiritual values rather than to the universally accepted Roman values is manifest. Environmentally the purity of the movement was damaged by the war and by subsequent dilution and exploitation. As an idea it is indestructible, progressing through the arts other than architecture and giving rise to the birth of a new art, that of collective landscape design.

Circle is introduced by the sculptor Naum Gabo, whose works were recently exhibited at the Tate Gallery in London in 1987, and whose lovely Constructional forms were ethereal and sublime. After describing the revolution in art and science at the beginning of the century and tracing the origins of Constructivism to Cubism, Gabo then explains the nature of this new phenomenon:

> The basis of the Constructivist idea in Art lies in an entirely new approach to the nature of Art and its functions in life. In it lies a complete reconstruction of the means in the different domains of Art, in the relations between them, in their methods and in their aims. It embraces those two functional elements on which Art is built up, namely, the Content and the Form. These two elements are from the Constructive point of view one and the same thing. It does not separate Content from Form — on the contrary, it does not see as possible their separated and independent existence. The thought that Form could have one designation and Content another cannot be incorporated in the concept of the Constructive idea. In a work of art they have to live and act as a unit, proceed in the same direction and produce the same effect. I say 'have to' because never before in

Le Corbusier's plan for Algiers, 1932

Art have they acted in such a way in spite of the obvious necessity of this condition. It has always been so in Art that either one or the other predominated, conditioning and predetermining the other.

This echoes the philosophy of Henry Moore's biological parallel Constructivist sculpture: that the invisible interior (the Content) is amalgamated with the visible exterior (the Form). This means that in architecture the body structure and façade are designed and comprehended as one. The concept proved disastrous for practitioners other than the artist-architect. The style became known as Functionalism which expressed the reality of the interior rather than the grander poetic conception of its idea; and the impact on society as a whole was horrendous.

Without question the pioneer of Constructivism in architecture was the painter-architect Le Corbusier. With most of his ideas too impractical in reality to be executed, and with all the subsequent aesthetic disasters laid at his door by posterity, yet history will continue to proclaim him one of the greatest innovators of an indestructible idea that the world has known. He is, in my view, closely followed by Berthold Lubetkin, in particular for his penguin pool at London Zoo and the elephant house at Birmingham —

sculptured forms in which lie the germ of modern landscape design.

What went wrong?

The first impression is that although Constructivism was based on machine production ('a home is a machine to live in' Corbusier is said to have said) and could add to the pleasures of existence in ways that the handicrafts could not, it did not in fact function so well. It was suitable for offices, factories and the like; it was too internationally anonymous to be expressive of public buildings and likewise — and most important of all — of the home. Primarily the shape was strange, lacking the familiarity that is an essence of a home. Materially the flat roofs proved less efficient than the pitched, and the white-rendered walls were costly to maintain or became shabby where bricks and stone were improved by time — at least as seen by the layman. Steel was cold whereas timber was warm to the touch. Tall blocks of dwellings that dramatically heralded the new age depended upon vulnerable mechanical lifts and other devices to exist at all. Gardens played little or no part. As if to emphasise the Constructive sense of flight and freedom from gravity the buildings were poised on pilotes, which made the ground wind-swept; and if they were not, a cluster created whirlwinds at the base. Neither sculptor nor painter need experience these devastating realities, nor need they necessarily feel the wrath of a client outraged by the mistakes, psychological as well as material.

These happenings would not by themselves have frustrated a movement in architecture that contained such a vital idea. In retrospect it seems clear that architectural thought, scholarship and the understanding of life in general,

Berthold Lubetkin's penguin pool, London Zoo, 1934. (Courtesy the Zoological Society of London)

Christopher Tunnard, gardens for St. Ann's Hill, Surrey

were restricted; and unlike sculpture and painting, this mattered. The restriction is exemplified in the two contrasting views on C G Jung by Henry Moore the biologist and Gabo the Constructivist. Moore's response on receiving a copy of Jung's *The Archetypal World of Henry Moore* was to read only the first chapter and then stop on the threshold of what seemed a vast unknown geography of the mind, whose exploration might inhibit his work as an artist. Gabo, on the other hand, speaking for Constructivism, would not accept that a deep subconscious existed at all. He wrote: 'Whatever is touched by Art becomes reality, and we do not need remote and distant navigation in the subconscioius in order to reveal a world which lies in our immediate vicinity.'

The subconscious as a factor in architecture cannot so easily be brushed aside. It is concerned with humans, their curious urges, their antecedents and a multitude of other complexities, such as the environment in which they live. Landscape design as recognised by Le Corbusier, for instance, was little more than a kind of abstract pseudo-romantic carpet upon which his buildings were to float.

The Constructivist movement was only one side of the coin of civilised life on this planet; the other, the complementary art of landscape design, was yet in its infancy.

While Le Corbusier evolved his own ideas of landscape; while Walter Gropius adopted the idea in a project for a giant block of flats to replace Blenheim Palace in its Capability Brown landscape; and while Christopher Tunnard struggled to find a domestic garden design suitable to Constructivism, yet land and landscape in the broader horizons remained little more than a vague idea. Constructivism is cold and hard and fashioned from the laws of the universe; the human animal is fashioned from earth and needs its sympathy and warmth.

Villa Capponi, Arcetri,
overlooking Florence

The Long Avenue, Villa
Gamberaia, Settignano

25

The reader will appreciate that these critical views have been formed long after the events. At the time I was unconcerned about the oddity of my dual practice, but was undoubtedly feeling the way towards creating an aesthetic status for landscape design and ultimately for amalgamation in my own mind of two equally distinguished modern arts. My garden practice consisted mainly in placing new gardens into old settings, which I did with technical and academic efficiency. It was not until the last decade, however, that I have appreciated the full philosophical significance to the modern age of the gardens of Mannerist Italy. So, let us wing our way to Florence, the birthplace of the concept that garden art can be personal as well as collective, and a statement on its own; let us for a short while absorb ourselves in this brief but fertile and prophetic age.

The period is undefined, but art historians agree that it lay between the end of the High Renaissance in the mid-sixteenth century and the Baroque that heralded the resurgence of the Church in the seventeenth century. In architecture the classical rules were no longer paramount and the professional was free to design according to the fancy of himself and his patron. The immediate and most memorable result was that the garden was no longer necessarily an extension of the villa and subservient to it. Closely welded though they were, and must always be, the garden had a mind of its own. Landscape was liberated from architecture.

Each garden was unique, not so much because it fitted the nature of its own terrain but because it reflected the mind or minds by which it was designed; and unlike the predetermined classical rules of architecture, no two individual minds can ever be alike. Certainly the minds of the Florentine family of Capponi were original and inventive. First, in 1570, they created the beautifully detailed asymmetrical gardens at Arcetri overlooking Florence, a simple design that has the archetypal similarities to Bingham's Melcombe in England; and in 1717 they finally synthesised and completed the slowly evolving complex of the Villa Gamberaia at Settignano across the Arno valley, whose concept of a domestic landscape is by general consent the most thoughtful the western world has known. It is significant that the long grass alley which finally co-ordinated the many parts into a single whole, was made long after the age of Mannerism was technically over and when the Church had returned to power to stamp out individuality and recapture the collective mind through the dramatic architecture of Baroque.

Portraiture flourished in Mannerist Florence. Artists like Agnolo Bronzino set out not only to immortalise the dignity of man but also the complex matters — the good, evil and indifferent — that make up the wholeness of his mind. The painter removes the mask of his sitter, studies what is behind, then returns the mask with such adjustment and distortion as may be necessary to reflect the interior. The process is a modified and more subtle form of Cubist portraiture, and it is not surprising that Surrealism itself seems to have been born in this liberal age.

According to Georgina Masson, writing of it in *Italian Gardens,* in 1961, the history of Gamberaia is obscure. An older villa was replaced by the present traditionally classical building in the late sixteenth century, probably including the terrace and the orthodox parterre water gardens. The argument is that this garden as it stands echoes almost every part of the human mind: the sensual, the practical, the contemplative, the mystical, the childish and, overall, the ordered grandeur of the individual. Operating through some unrecorded architect or architects whose professionalism was immaculate, the Capponi family were able to create an environment whose ethos was an extension of its own deepest feelings. The unknown architect himself is like a portrait painter who records not only the visible and conscious of his sitter, but also the invisible and subconscious.

It was in this lack of understanding of human nature, whose structure is more complex than the cosmos, that the Constructivist genius of the 1930s was deficient. But there were exceptions that give us a vision of what might have been had there not been a war.

When you stand on a certain grass spot on the higher part of Kenwood that lies between the Hampstead and Highgate heights in northern London, you will see a vision of the brave new world of the 'thirties. You must choose a sunny summer evening. The green slopes away in front of you to disappear into a valley. On either side are the trees of Kenwood Park. The eighteenth century mansion itself is out of sight to the left, and so too is the great broken bronze of Henry Moore. In the far distance and on the rising skyline you see what at first appears to be the fairy-like white castle that we see in medieval prints. It is, in reality, the block of flats called Highpoint, designed by Berthold Lubetkin in the mid-'thirties and lying on the original Great North Road just north of Highgate Village. It is the conception of an environment that is indeed the vision of a brave new world. I know because I live there.

Wartime housing, Theale, Berkshire

DECADE 1940-1950:
THE EMERGENCE OF
MODERN LANDSCAPE DESIGN

In war the creative subconscious is frozen by the conscious in action. Yet there can be localised thaws, and with me they would occur during the long hours of fire-watching at night. My watch was divided equally between a team in central London and myself alone with my wife at home in north London. During the first, and while others passed the time usually in playing cards, I would make my own personal sketch details for several war-cum-peace housing projects for which I was responsible — a feat quite impossible on the triple-speed drawing board of the day time. At home I became absorbed in the classics, topping up my existing knowledge of English novelists with those that were foreign. The Russians were a revelation, for it seemed to me that whereas the reader was an observer of happenings in an English novel, in the Russian he was a partaker in an extra dimension. Stranded today on a desert island with a choice of four books apart from Shakespeare and the Bible, I would choose, in order of preference: Dostoievski, Proust, Thomas Mann and V S Naipaul, none of whom are English. In all these the subconscious dominates and directs the conscious.

The war was over. The call for the reconstruction of Britain to make her a land fit for heroes was overwhelming. A great non-party army of statesmen, politicians, academics and professionals acted as one to try and realise this ideal. Overnight the concept of landscape design emerged from obscurity to create a vital profession. To unfreeze the batteries and recharge them my wife and I went to Sweden to absorb the new architecture and landscape of which we had heard, and to eat as much smoked salmon as we were able. Among the revelations of the new Stockholm was the work of Gunnar Asplund. I was deeply moved; after the militant and single-mindedness of the Constructivists, Asplund's work was gently reassuring. I quote from *The Landscape of Man:*

> A pure Classicist rather than a Mannerist, Asplund's objective was two-fold: to discard superficial style and re-create the essence of Classicism in a modern language: and to harmonise geometric values with those of landscape... Although the structure of the lay-out [of the Woodland Cemetery] is geometric and proportioned, the whole is subordinate to the artificial hill. The hill, concealing an adjoining suburb, is a universal and timeless symbol complementing the Christian cross, which is particular.

Until now Gaudier-Brzeska and Asplund were the only two Modernists to move me as passionately as the traditional arts. Now there was to be a third experience through sculpture. Henry Moore had always mystified me as to why his distorted forms were so highly acclaimed by critics whose judgement I respected. Then one day that I shall long remember, I visited an exhibition of modern sculpture in Battersea Park. On a slight grass hillock the 'Three Standing Figures' were illuminated in the low sunlight. I was aghast. I knew all.

Frederick Gibberd now enters the scene.

Gibberd had followed me earlier as principal of the turbulent school of architecture of the Architectural Association. He was a 'thirties Constructivist

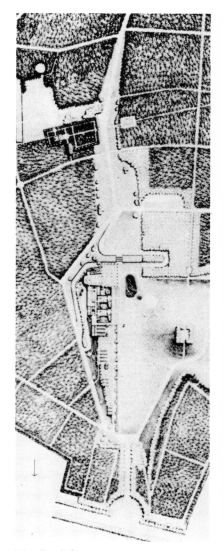

Woodland Cemetery, Stockholm, as existing in 1940

with the edges softened by scholarship, and was to become one of the leading architects with a cathedral, a mosque, Heathrow Airport and countless buildings of all kinds to his credit; *and* the basic plan for the new town of Harlow in Essex. It was this latter project of 1946 that was to transform my aesthetics and point the way to ultimate depths that I never ever knew existed.

This is how it happened.

Gibberd had become a close friend and neighbour in an eighteenth century house similar to my own in Grove Terrace, north London. The interiors were identical in plan and each had a charming historic front. We both had interesting pictures, but while mine were representational and included the Chinese, his were prints of unintelligible scrawls and sketches by artists only vaguely known to me, such as squiggles by a Paul Klee and amateur's geometry by Ben Nicholson (whom I had once met and been trounced). In 1946 Gibberd and I were each appointed on the same day to prepare and

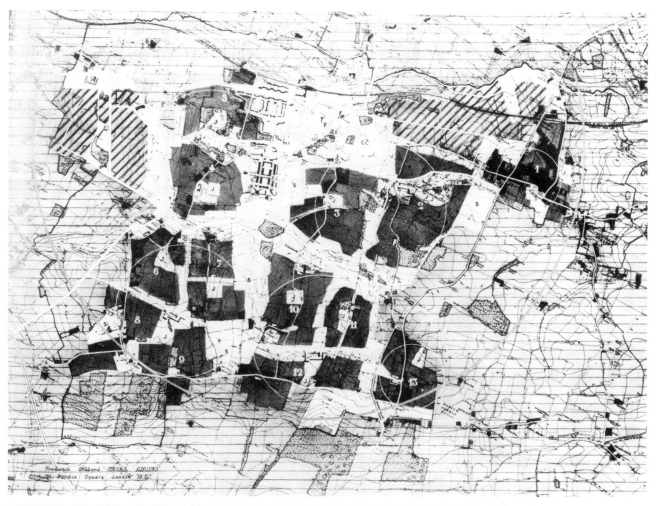

First plan for Harlow New
Town, Essex, by Frederick
Gibberd

Ben Nicholson, 'Mousehole',
1947

complete plans, in one year, for the new towns of Hemel Hempstead and Harlow, myself as senior having the choice.

The plans were finished to time and exhibited separately on the same day. Harlow was acclaimed by the critics; Hemel Hempstead was not (being later re-planned by the Corporation itself). The Harlow plan was realised in thirty-five years, virtually without change. What was the elixir in Gibberd's plan that gave it life when mine was born dead? There were two reasons, one of the conscious and the other of the subconscious. The conscious error of Hemel Hempstead was that, like classical Edinburgh, the core had to be completed without change; it was inorganic, whereas the Harlow plan was organic and could grow freely as does a plant with pruning but without clipping. The subconscious error was that the Hemel Hempstead plan did not reflect the liberal ethos of the time whereas Harlow, in a strikingly beautiful plan seemingly inspired by the painter Ben Nicholson, undoubtedly did. I realised that in some way Gibberd was drawing inspiration from his pictures. 'They pour electricity into me', he later said.

And so, at the age of fifty, I began to try to push wider open the door to the unknown of which I had had a glimpse through sculpture. I visited galleries and browsed endlessly in books on individual abstract or near-abstract painters. Then, like a thunderbolt from on high came Picasso. It is through painting alone that from now on I shall take you, the reader, upon a voyage into a world of the subsconscious that seems to me to be infinite in its powers to inspire the visible world. The purpose of the exercise is to suggest how these powers can be extracted, translated and transmitted to landscape design.

This journey into the underworld will be more pleasant than that of Virgil and Dante into the Inferno but it will have a certain similarity in its probing of the character and mind of the great artists, dead or living. The paintings and drawings are presented in the same chronological order in which I made my discoveries; the order is inconsequential, since the subconscious knows no time nor place. Unless otherwise stated, the pictures are on my walls or in my books. So off we go.

Pablo Picasso, from 'Variations on Velazquez' The Maids of Honour', 1957

DECADE 1950-1960:
THE UNDERWORLD OF ART

The descent into an artist's subconscious through his paintings is open to all who respond to his art. What is not clear is the means by which a landscape designer can draw inspiration from this underground wealth of ideas. As a method and simple example let us take a Picasso plate and metamorphose it into landscape reality.

You, the landscape designer, have been asked to design a 'giardino segreto' in an existing woodland glade through which runs a rivulet. The programme is not unusual and any reasonable solution could not fail to be attractive — wild flowers, water plants, possibly a statuette of Pan, and so forth. The client may be satisfied, but are you yourself? Is there not something trivial about the

Pablo Picasso plate

result, something that belongs more to a popular flower show than a work of art that appeals to mind as well as eye?

You turn to art books you may possess, and if you have only one, let it be (as a landscape designer) *Beyond Appearance* by C H Waddington, Edinburgh University Press; but there should be others to give you a wide range. You browse through the illustrations, each of which is an acknowledged work of art

with its own abstract foundation. You will note the figurative subject, if there is one, for it may come to suggest further ideas; but you are really searching for something that will strike a chord in your own subconscious. The intellect cannot advise you and should be ignored.

Suddenly you pause before a Picasso plate. Something has stirred within you. By all means take note that it shows a woman's face, but what has held you is the beautiful abstract composition. Your imagination now converts it into a woodland-garden scene: the strong white line which dominates the composition becomes an architectural feature whose flowing waters have emerged from the banks of the glade.

And now, with Paul Nash to see us off and attended by eminent critics, we will enter the world of the subconscious.

Paul Nash, 'Trees'
From the earliest days of his career Nash seems to have possessed a peculiar liking for fences as a feature of the landscape. While they undoubtedly served to accentuate the ordered character of the countryside with which Nash was familiar and, perhaps indirectly, to represent man's part in the shaping of it, they had from the outset a formal rather than an illustrative significance. This is proved, I think, by his fondness for introducing other constructive features of a similar kind. E.H. Ramsden,
Paul Nash

Graham Sutherland, 'Figure with Tree'
His great contribution, it seems to me, has been his discovery of pictorial images which should assist us to bridge the gap imaginatively between the separate realms of the human, the organic and the mechanical. Douglas Cooper, Graham Sutherland

Graham Sutherland, 'Boulder and Lane', 1940
Sutherland succumbed visually and emotionally to the ambience in what he calls his 'voluptuous awareness' [which] comes into play and releases his pictorial inspiration. Moreover, having found a locality which appeals to him, Sutherland allows himself to be obsessed by it and goes back in order to try and 'pin down the essence' more exactly. For he is haunted by a desire that the forms, lines and colours in his pictures shall really conjure up 'the essence of the likeness' to that particular place. Douglas Cooper, Graham Sutherland

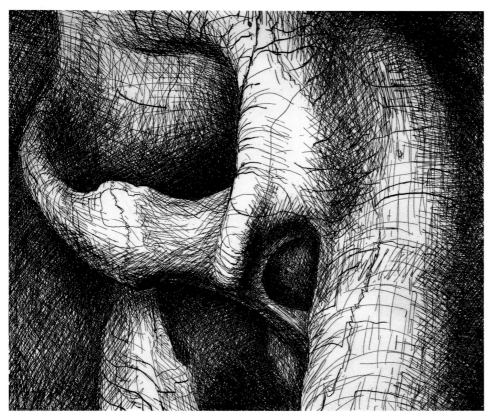

Henry Moore, 'Dark Etching', c.1950
Moore wrote: 'The observation of nature is part of an artist's life; it enlarges his form-knowledge, keeps him fresh and from working only by formula, and feeds inspiration.' While admitting that the human figure interested him 'most deeply', he added 'I have found principles of forms and rhythm from the study of natural objects such as pebbles, rocks, bones, trees, plants etc.' For Moore human forms were now latent in nature: the study of a jaw bone . . .

Henry Moore, 'Reclining Figure', 1931
. . . could result in a reclining figure. In addition, the juxtaposition of new forms derived from stones or shaped wood could convey tensions of attraction or dependence. . . He took the role of the 'subsconscious part of the mind' for granted. 'There are universal shapes to which everybody is subsconsciously conditioned and to which they can respond if their conscious control does not shut them off.' Susan Compton, Henry Moore

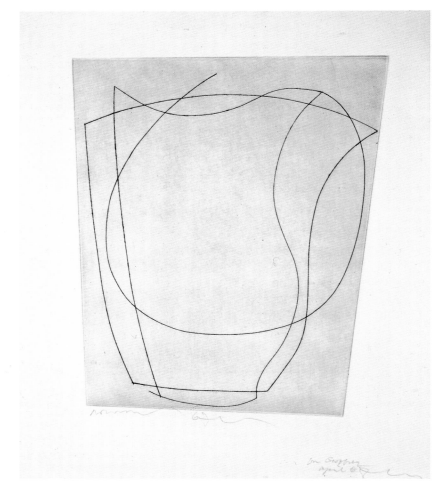

Ben Nicholson, 'Jugs', c.late
1930s
What is special about Ben
Nicholson is, in fact, the
continuous overlapping of his
ideas. We can find in the
work an idea of landscape, an
idea of architecture, an idea
of the human figure and an
idea of art. These ideas do
not come separately. They are
not arranged in series or in
tiers. None has precedence
over the others. The work is
all of them, simultaneously.
Architecture, then. Nicholson
responds as much as anyone
to the . . .

Ben Nicholson, 'Dome'
. . . grand organ-music of
space as it was realised by
Alberti or Palladio, or in the
Court of Honour in the Ducal
Palace at Urbino. But, once
again, the particular breaks
in. Faced with an intrusive
telegraph wire, or a gull that
won't give up its perch, or a
bit of dead wall that simply
shouldn't be there, Nicholson
puts them all in and somehow
gets them to rhyme with the
sublime statements that first
prompted the drawings. John
Russell, Ben Nicholson

André Masson, 'Figures'
[*Masson*] *was a highly cerebral artist who developed a personal mythology with great purity, energy and restlessness of line. In 1947 he settled in Provence and found a new style of landscape which has been compared to the deep spiritual rapport with nature which is reflected in some Chinese paintings.* The Oxford Companion to Art

Accompanying this bitter pessimism is a passionate hope, through painting, to be able to find and express the mysterious unity of the universe hinted at in primitive myths and religions. H H Arnason, A History of Modern Art

DECADE 1960-1970:
THE UNDERWORLD OF ART
(continued)

We emerge from the underworld and take stock of what we have with us. It is clear from *Jung and the Art of Landscape* (Volume IV), that my designs were already inspired mainly by Paul Klee, Henry Moore and Ben Nicholson. Although these explorations into the roots of design were light-hearted, they indicated that I was convinced of something of the utmost importance to the arts: however indecisive may be the conscious visible design by the artist, his subconscious is decisive in its urge towards perfection. This impulse is individual, collective and universal.

With Klee and Moore as luminaries it was easy enough to transpose

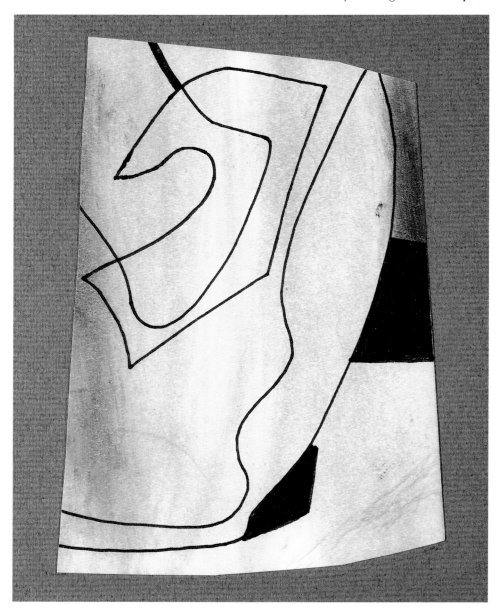

Ben Nicholson, 'Small Abstract', 1979 [Nicholson's] art seems to stand apart from that of the continent. . . The difference is difficult to define; it may have something to do with Nicholson's continuing feeling for objective nature, his particular feeling for line, or perhaps some intangible in the English tradition. H H Arnason, A History of Modern Art

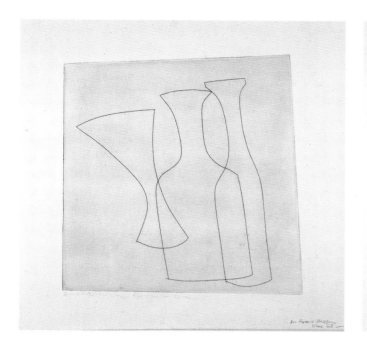

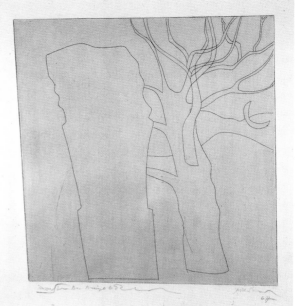

landscape into a shape inspired by animal, vegetable or human form — shapes generally recognised to be as close to perfection as this planet permits. To avoid sentimentality this metamorphosis of life into land should remain a secret, a 'feeling' rather than a picture-story. Ben Nicholson remains inscrutable and to this day I do not understand the charm and sense of power that emanates from his work. Let us look at him more closely, for he has been my greatest mentor.

Consider the abstract opposite, willed by Ben Nicholson to my wife and myself towards the end of the seventh decade. It is abstract and to the intellect totally unintelligible; yet it seems to contain a whole world of intangible ideas that so far have eluded translation. What is this magic that is beyond rational comprehension? Nicholson's range was vast. For myself, the power of the geometric reliefs (drawn to the minutest degree of balance) are comprehensible, for clearly the intellect responds to the beauty of proportion. What is not comprehensible is why a grossly distorted drawing of a building should make it look more real than reality; why trivial bottles should acquire heroic stature; and why trees become symbolic of one knows not what (when asked why the branches of the tree above did not appear on the further side of the obstacle, Nicholson briefly replied 'that's the point.' Usually he replied to questions on the meaning of his drawings 'how should *I* know?').

In 1963 came the commission for the Kennedy Memorial at Runnymede, and for the first time I was challenged to take seriously the concept of the subconscious. Was it possible to bury a great invisible idea within a modest visible world? I now turned to literature for help and found in Bunyan's *Pilgrim's Progress* the study of Life, Death and Spirit; and this majestic saga, unseen and unrecognisable intellectually, is embodied in the landscape.

Grappling with forces of the subconscious that might be figments of my imagination, I now sought out Jung for guidance, and found it. With the knowledge confirmed that the subconsciouis within us lives a life independent of the conscious, we now re-enter this strange land of shadows.

Ben Nicholson, 'Bottles', 1968
Often, when I was alone, I sat down on this stone and then began an imaginary game that went something like this: 'I am sitting on top of this stone and it is underneath.' But the stone could also say 'I' and think: 'I am lying here on this slope and he is sitting on top of me.' The question then arose: 'Am I the one who is sitting on the stone on which he is sitting?'...

Ben Nicholson, 'Tree', 1967
... This question always perplexed me and I would stand up wondering who was what now. The answer remained totally unclear, and my uncertainty was accompanied by a feeling of curious and fascinating darkness. But there was no doubt whatsoever that this stone stood in some secret relationship to me. I could sit on it for hours, fascinated by the puzzle it set me. C J Jung, Memories, Dreams, Reflections

41

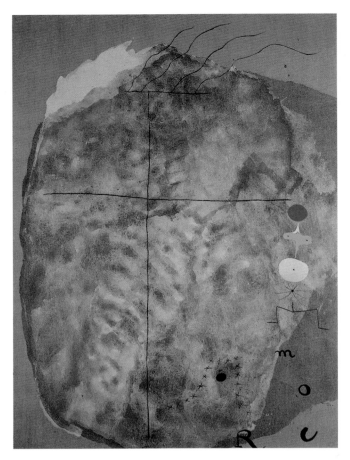

Joan Miro, 'Amour', 1926
Devoid as they are of any realistic connotation, Miro's compositions suggest above all a will to metamorphose, the result of that myth-making propensity which characterises the romantic mind. It was Gericault who said 'I set out to make a picture of a woman and it ends up as a lion,' and similarly the fauns and centaurs of mythology started off with human forms before being metamorphosed into hybrid, half-animal beings. Maurice Raynal, Modern Painting

Above right: Paul Klee, 'The Order of the High C', 1921
Klee had no difficulty in breaking loose from a material environment which he studied only for its own sake only at the very outset of his career as an artist; and he soon discovered his vocation: that of initiating us into that peculiar world of his whose wonders and delights unfurled themselves increasingly upon the screen of his vivid imagination. Maurice Raynal, Modern Painting

Joan Miro, 'Maternity', 1924
Miro seizes on the most significant details of his subject and isolates them so as to give them greater emphasis. In 'Maternity' these are the mother's breast and the child, which figure in opposite corners of the picture, seen full face and in profile. Fine-spun delicate lines ensure the continuity between the various elements and assign each its place in space. Maurice Raynal, Modern Painting

Paul Klee, 'Senecio', 1922
We used to represent things visible on earth, things we enjoyed seeing. Now we reveal the underlying reality of visible things and thus express our belief that visible reality is merely an isolated phenomenon, outnumbered by other, unseen realities. Thus things take on a vaster, more varied significance, often seemingly in contradiction with rational experience. Hence a tendency to stress the element of the essential in the random. Maurice Raynal, Modern Painting

Jackson Pollock, 'Alchemy', 1947 (Peggy Guggenheim Collection)
Aside from their intrinsic quality, Pollock's drip paintings contributed other elements that changed the course of modern painting. There was first the concept of the overall painting, the painting seemingly without beginning or end, extending to the very limits of the canvas and implying an extension even beyond. This, together with the large scale of the works, introduced another concept — that of wall painting different from the tradition of easel painting, even as it existed in cubism and geometric abstraction.

This was the final break from the Renaissance idea of painting detached from spectator, to be looked at as a self-contained unit. The painting became an environment, an ensemble, which encompassed the spectator, surrounding him on all sides. The feeling of absorption or participation is heightened by the ambiguity of the picture space. The colours and lines, although never puncturing the space, still create an illusion of continuous movement, a billowing, a surging back and forth, within a limited depth. H H Arnason, A History of Modern Art

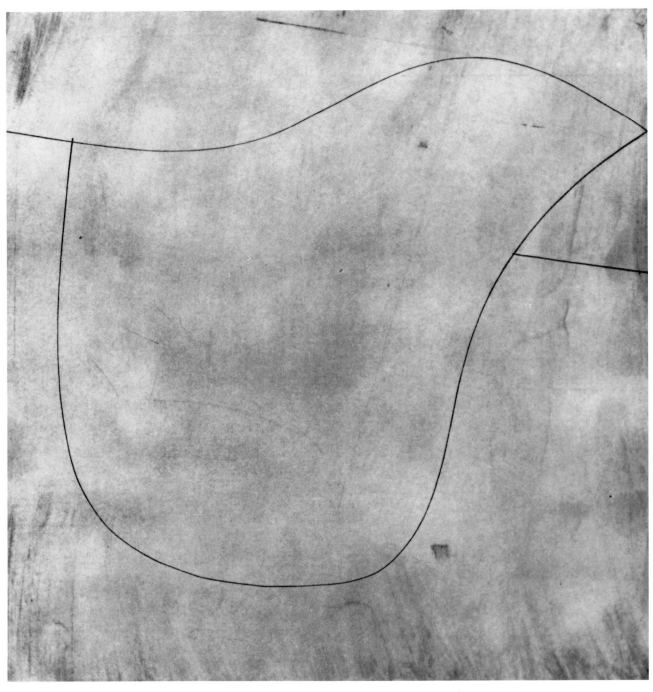

Ben Nicholson, 'Bull Frog', 1962
Jung and the subconscious were quietly put to rest, sleeping peacefully

DECADE 1970-1980:
INTERLUDE

With three score years and ten behind me and a practice in decline and decay, it seems inevitable that I should have retired from active business in favour of a quiet life at home. The decade was to be almost wholly devoted to the contemplation of the why and the wherefore of life as a generality and the art of landscape as a particular. After an active life in the arts, the urge was now to seek out beginnings and study their significance to the modern world. Jung and the subconscious were quietly laid to rest, sleeping peacefully.

Because my wife, Susan, and I had always in the past travelled for two purposes only — either to attend a conference of the International Federation of Landscape Architects, or to examine *in situ* material for *The Landscape of Man* — or both — we had never actually soaked in the present and past allurements of the Mediterranean. We now seemed inexorably drawn, like countless others, to the landscapes and waters of that mighty cradle of western civilisation. Although the visits were only for an annual fortnight, they built up a stirring Odyssey in the imagination, regardless of sequence and time. Let us briefly glance at this Odyssey, for it proved a spring-board for the future.

First to the Italian lakes: to Maggiore with Isola Bella drifting on its waters like some celestial barge, and to Como of which long ago my father had said 'see Como and die.' Now to the Isles of Greece, where burning Sappho loved and sung; to Corfu, Aegina and Crete, where Zeus' cavern on Mount Aegeum proved too stiff a climb for us old things; to Mykonos and the floating island of Delos, birthplace of Apollo, god of light and many other things as well. Thence back over the wine-red waters to Majorca and Sicily. In Taormina, February 1975, on a public seat within the majestic landscape of Mount Etna and the long white sea-shore leading to Catania, I wrote the final paragraph of *The Landscape of Man:*

> For the first time in history the shape of the world that is unfolding expresses collective materialism rather than prescribed religion. In the advanced countries the individual is evolving his own personal beliefs within his own home. The greatest threat to his existence may not be commercialism, or war, or pollution or noise or consumption of capital resources, or even the fear of extinction from without, but rather the blindness that follows sheer lack of appreciation and the consequent destruction of those values in history that together are symbolic of a single great idea.

Mount Etna and the sea, land and water, the hard and the soft, the *Yang* and the *Yin* — we were experiencing this basic structure of the visible world in its grandest and most significant form. As if to express the spirit of this structure as well as that of the decade itself, and to prepare the reader for the explosive seventh decade, there follows an extract from *Water,* initiated and illustrated by my wife and scripted by me.

The Nature of Water

In England there is already so much water that its virtues are apt to be taken for granted. We ourselves are made of it: for as H.G. Wells puts it, 'all living things, plants and animals alike, are primarily water things'. Without it we could not live for more than a few days: with it we can survive, create civilisations, play with it and make works of art to express the joy of living.

This book is concerned with the poetry of water in the making of landscape and architecture and of fantasy of all kinds. Its uses have made endless artificial patterns on the surface of the earth and these in turn have enriched our lives through art and philosophy. Such a pattern may be anything from a formal little garden rill to the outline of a whole city. The examples are selected from all subjects and from all parts of the world, ranging from Hadrian's Villa in the Roman Campagna below Tivoli to Sea City in the North Sea, and from the Summer Palaces in Peking to Chapultepec Park in Mexico City.

The oldest and perhaps the most spectacular natural water architecture is also that which has had scarcely any influence as an art form. This is the subterranean stalactite cavern, without light and lifeless. Man could never have emerged from this and therefore has no desire to return to it by emulating its form. Perhaps there is some affinity with the complexities of an Arab ceiling, but this may be accounted for by a different feeling: a desire to counteract and escape from the blinding immensity of the Middle East sky.

It is from scenes like the river landscape opposite that man as an amphibian emerged many millions of years ago to crawl ashore and start a habitat on land. The subconscious appeal to return to water seems to increase the more his daily life becomes remote from his beginnings. This urge towards the sea began most noticeably in Britain at the coming of the industrial age, with the creation of

'The underlying attraction of the movement of water and sand seems to be biological'. River estuary, Kentra Bay, Argyllshire

Brighton and other seaside resorts. Today he flies to the warmer waters of the Mediterranean.

The underlying attraction of the movement of water and sand therefore seems to be biological. If we look more deeply we can see it as the basis of an abstract idea linking ourselves with the limitless mechanics of the universe: man has always stretched out to the infinite. Note his little endeavours on land, mainly of tree-planting; the tiny indentations of the cliffs, works of nature with which he had nothing to do but with which he is closely associated; and compare these with the splendid sweep of the water on its way to the sea. We can then begin to understand why some of the curious shapes of modern art, otherwise unintelligible, should have such appeal. The subconscious within us has sensed an affinity with something that is in direct opposition to the mechanical sciences and is on a greater scale than ourselves.

The laws of nature created from water the first scientific piece of hard sculpture — the shell. Shells are not works of art as we recognise the term, but rather works of organic engineering. Their perfection is absolute. Perhaps more than any other animal shape they have moulded our sense of beauty. They are based on geometry, but biologically and not mathematically. Their shapes repeat, but not exactly. It must be admitted that while man with his hands and his instruments has created richer and more meaningful objects, he has never achieved the variety and consistent perfection of form that arise from this sculpture from the sea bed.

Giant clam (Tridacna gigas Lamarckii). *Shell forms have often provided the basis for the designs of fountains*

The chasm at Tivoli from a drawing by W Havell, c.1850, a landscape created by the action of water

It was a considerable time in the evolution of *Homo sapiens* before the first works of art based on water began to appear. First, man the animal needed to provide himself with food and shelter and protection. He was driven to seek refuge in caves, but rarely in those that were damp and uncomfortable with stalagmites. The first art appeared in the primitive cave drawings and these were of land animals, with here and there a fish. The drawings were concerned with magic and, lovely though they are, it is significant that the authors of them should not have included the movement of water for its own sake. This was to come later.

The Temple of the Sybil, Tivoli, today. Before the diversion of the water the temple stood immediately above the cascade

Whether we are watching the ceaseless movement of the waves on the seashore or the eddies on the surface of a pool, or reflections on a calm day, the fascination of water seems almost timeless. It is romantic: romance liberates the imagination and relieves frustrations. These emotions are not peculiar to our age and it is rewarding to look back at the golden ages of history and see how men reacted in circumstances not dissimilar to our own.

In classical Rome, for instance, was there an endeavour to balance the dictator's genius for law and order with the poetic, the rational with the irrational? The age certainly expressed gentle human emotions through poets such as Horace and Virgil, whose works are redolent of the countryside. Occasionally it did so in landscape itself, although the direct impact of the works of the state upon landscape was usually one of domination. Fortunately, there still exists a landscape that seems to reflect the poetic spirit of Rome rather than that of its emperors. This is the chasm at Tivoli, crowned by the Temple of the Sybil. It is a landscape that has been created by the action of water, and above all one that has been lifted into the sublime by a single man-made but godlike object. The temple proclaims the harmony of the universe, giving meaning to the great turbulent scene above which it is poised.

It is said that a Roman emperor retired to Tivoli to cure insomnia by sleeping within sound of the falls. Today the waters immediately below the temple have been diverted to create electric power, but the rocks of the original course remain like some mighty works of sculpture (overleaf). Cascades continue to crash nearby, the trees and shrubs cling hazardously to their rocks and it is still possible to recreate in imagination and in emotion the stupendous scene as it was in antiquity. In a sense the Temple of the Sybil is a stepping-stone for man on his progress from sea bed to eternity.

*Rock forms at Tivoli caused
by water erosion and giving
inspiration to the sculptor*

The cascade at Tivoli

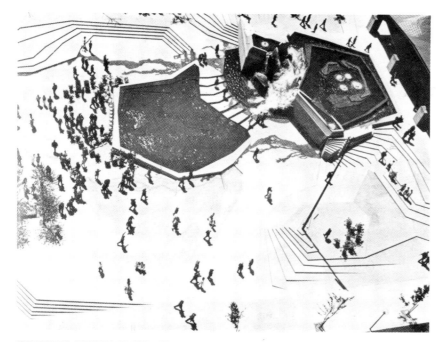

Lovejoy Plaza, Portland, Oregon, USA, general view and detail. The inspiration came from the mountain waterfalls of the High Sierras. Laurence Halpin, landscape architect

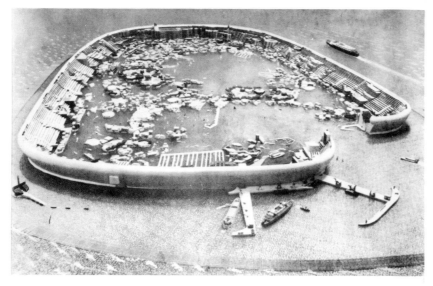

Sea City, 1968, a project for a human water habitat off the coast of Norfolk. The flats in which most people would live are built into the outer wall. Public buildings would be on the floating islands in the central lagoon. Hal Moggridge, landscape designer

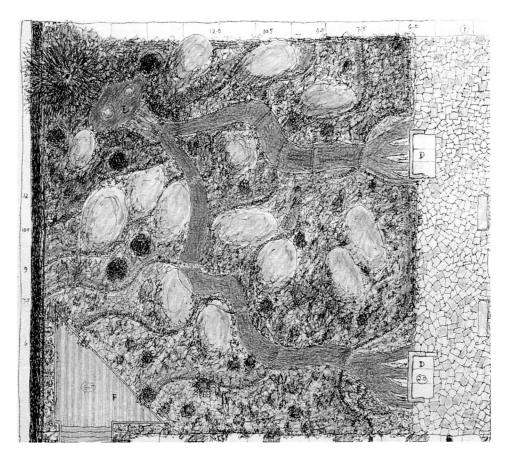

To the intellect the drawing by Paul Klee (below) is unintelligible; the appeal is to the subconscious. Such was the inspiration for the bodiless water figure among boulders (right and below right), drawings of part of the nineteenth century rock garden at the proposed Moody Historical Gardens, Galveston, Texas. Note the head with its bubble-fountain eyes, the long arms with fingers clutching the balconies. It will not be consciously recognisable as such to the visitor, but subconsciously it will. It symbolises the uncertainty lying beneath the Victorian High Civilisation. Geoffrey Jellicoe, The Landscape of Civilisation

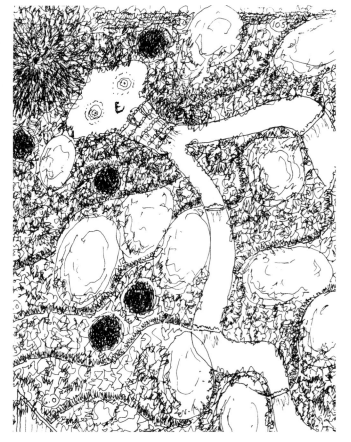

DECADE 1980-1990:
FANTASIA

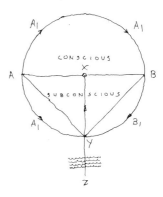

Post-Jungian diagram suggesting the creative process in landscape design, 1988

A   *A Client*
A1   *Client's instructions*
B   *Designer*
B1   *Designer's first thoughts*
Y   *Joint subconscious*
Z   *Deep subconscious*
X   *Final design*

During the decade I was commissioned to design and partially detail gardens and landscape whose costs in the aggregate were more than a thousand times the sum of all my previous works in this field. It is no wonder that I advised lecture audiences that life begins not at forty, as they might suppose, but at eighty.

Thoughts on Jung quickly revived and I now felt confident to prepare a post-Jungian diagram showing how this concept of the subconscious could extend to the creation of landscape design. Jung himself does not seem to have explored the relation of psyche to environment other than to make a deep study of the alchemist and the experience of his own home beside Lake Zurich.

Let us now relax and enjoy this seventh decade with a glance at some of the fantasies that have emerged to distort from a practical background of planning, drawing and detailing, and consider from where they might have come. There is no suggestion that they can themselves stand comparison with the originals.

René Magritte, 'The Knowledge', 1961
Magritte. . . sought to reveal an inner, poetic meaning of objects in the external environment by setting them in startling and disturbing juxtapositions, creating disassociation which embodies a half-intellectual element of suggestion. Intelligence, sensitivity and imagination combine in his works, which he regarded as an instrument of knowledge, though knowledge not reducible to conceptualisation. Oxford Companion to Art

Sutton Place, Homage to the Magnolia, 1982
An existing magnolia being too small and tender in itself to terminate a very long vista, was framed in a window and heralded by three monster Roman vases that were incongruous in the domestic landscape. The purpose is to disorientate the mind by a deliberate incongruity in the juxtaposition of disparate objects, preparing it for the tranquillity of the great Nicholson Wall reached through a green tunnel on the left

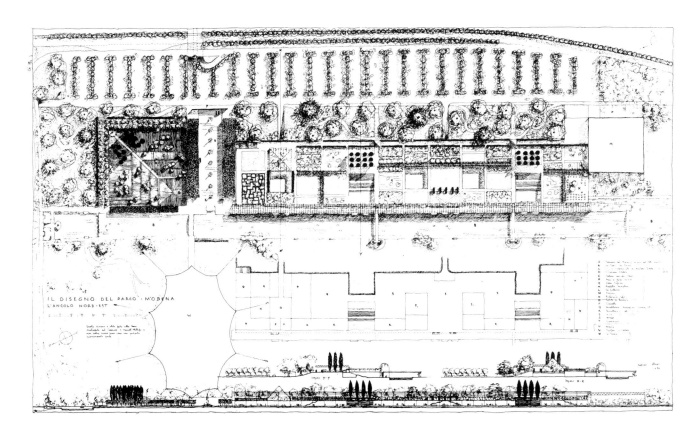

Project for Civic Park, Modena, Italy, 1984
Visibly *the park is to provide recreation and relief, like any town park, for a collective urban society.* Invisibly *it is intended to reinforce the values of the old city by opening the windows of the subconscious upon the dignity and relevance of the classical world. Geoffrey and Susan Jellicoe,* The Landscape of Man

Georgio Di Chirico, 'The Uncertainty of the Poet', 1913
. . . *the wistful nostalgic atmosphere of a world in which the impossible mingles with the possible and whose time and space are other than the time and space of the real world. There is, in fact, a creation of that 'inner eye', that faculty of visualising worlds beyond one's own, common to poets and children. Maurice Raynal,* Modern Painting

56

Piet Mondrian, 'Composition in Red, Yellow and Blue', 1927
Speaking at the Paul Klee commemoration in Berne in 1940, Michael Seuphor, author of Mondrian, said 'Among the greatest contemporary artists, the Spaniard Picasso is the most tremendous vital force, the Dutchman Piet Mondrian the most fundamental constructive force, and the German, Paul Klee the profoundest explorer of reality'

Sports Park Centre, Turin, March 1989
Until this commission, Mondrian had been the only artist of world and architectural reputation to whom I could not respond. His abstracts seemed lifeless and pointless. The site of the proposed Turin sports park, however, is part of the city grid-iron plan, and because of the multiple-use programme it was instinctively to Mondrian I turned for help to secure order out of chaos with a classical grandeur of conception. The plan was rejected and, overleaf, a romantic solution proposed one year later

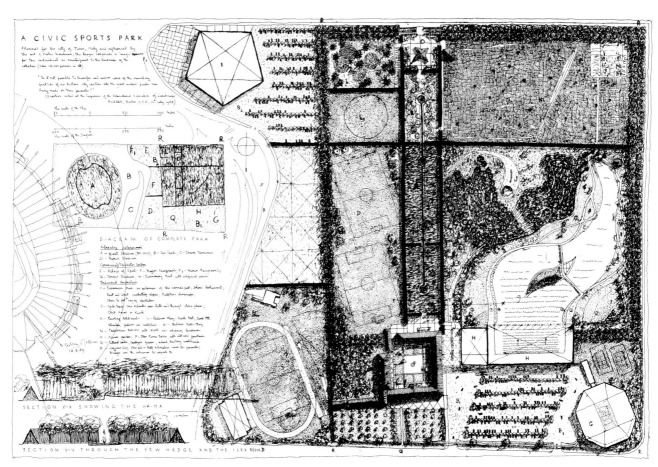

A CIVIC SPORTS PARK

Pablo Picasso, Cover to 'Variations on Velazquez' The Maids of Honour', 1957

Sports Park Centre, Turin, March 1990
A year after the submission of the Turin plan of 1989, the architect in charge, Pietro Derossi, proposed coming to London to show me his alternative idea on which I was to be asked to collaborate. Unless his proposal adopted the principal of segregation of collective (i.e. spectators and cars) from individual sport, I was not interested. He came, I saw and was conquered. He had spread a landscape carpet over the whole site with the structures swept beneath its ruffles. How to compose this oddity with its loose ends into a harmonious whole? As we left my study I picked up Picasso's 'Variations on Velazquez' The Maids of Honour' and there, on the cover, was the answer

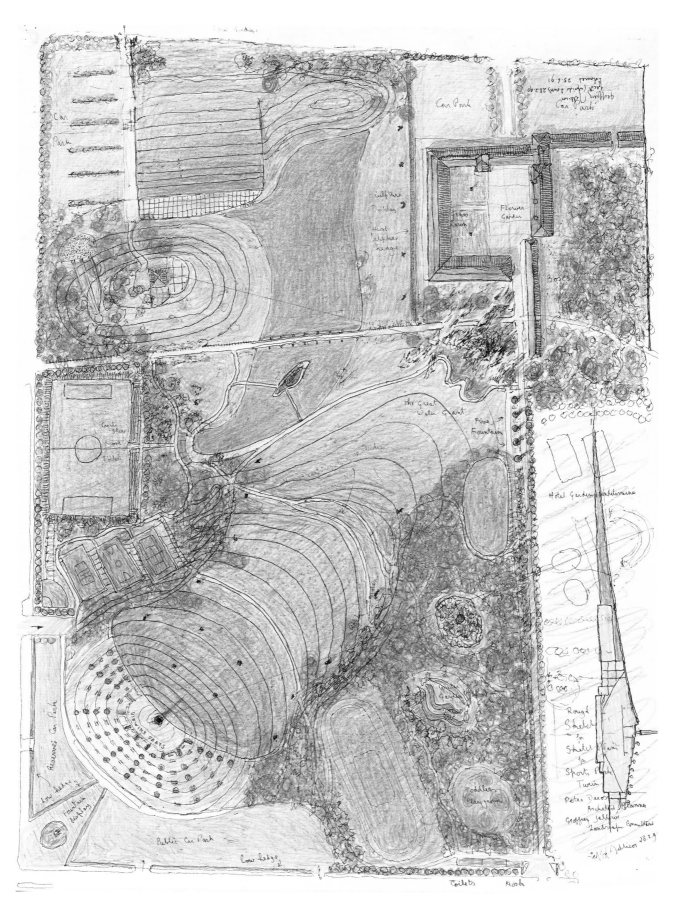

59

DECADE 1990:
POSTSCRIPT FOR HERACLITUS

It might be thought that an eighth decade would be concerned with matters other than professional practice. On the contrary there has been opened up a vision of landscape far beyond that of the personal. It is the vision of a whole country unified by landscape design, the laboratory being the Atlanta Historical Society and the guiding hand the Greek philosopher Heraclitus, 500 B.C.

It seems appropriate to conclude this introduction to the four volumes of my writings with the *Meditation in the Grove of Heraclitus* which also terminates Volume IV. The 'fire' refers to the American Civil War disaster of 1864. Heraclitus wrote 'Beginnings and ends are shared in the circumference of a circle'. So we, too, will begin at the beginning, travel round the circle, and return to where we began.

A Meditation: In the Grove of Heraclitus

We have just passed through the pleasant gardens of the twentieth century, experienced a sinister landscape, climbed from darkness to the great terrace, and so into the grove of Heraclitus. Here let us pause and ruminate on our passage through time and space. We are now in the company of an irritable old man of some twenty-five centuries, a philosopher who declared that 'fire is need and satiety' and 'war is the father of all', and would be so for ever (perhaps he was right and let us hope that future wars will be economic and that fire will be as creative as the one we have just experienced). Although insulting both Homer and Pythagoras, and seemingly hostile to the human race as a whole, our companion is nevertheless being accepted as the father of modern metaphysics. Before exploring this new idea, and ignoring the protests of our companion, let us first make an appreciation of the classical triumphs that were 'the glory that was Greece and the grandeur that was Rome'.

The declaration of Heraclitus that all things were in flux could not be denied – indeed it was obvious – and it was to provide a sense of stability essential to the human race that Plato evolved the theory of ideas. Plato the mathematician and Aristotle the biologist were concerned only with rational thought and pure reason. They opposed myth and mysticism, and the subconscious as a scientific study and source of deduction did not come their way. Deduction from observation conceived the cosmos to be mathematical, absolute and eternal. The circle, where the end is the beginning, was the mother figure. Could not this divine concept be transmitted to earth to breathe divinity into man's work? Pythagoras had already discovered an affinity between the music of the spheres and that of man, and why not with the other arts? Hence were evolved those abstract mathematical proportions that fill us with wonder, reassurance and placidity. The rub is that today things are not what had been imagined. Plato's noble conception of a metaphysical link between man and eternity has been broken by the scientist. Can the artist repair and renew the link?

All artists are subconsciously struggling to reach the perfection that is not of this world. The romantic artist seeks for it in things on earth or in the clouds above; the classical artist has sought for it in the cosmos beyond the skies. Now that the conception of cosmic stability is no more, to what ends are the artists groping? Can romanticism, the art of change, metamorphose itself into an art that could be called cosmic?

And so we come to Heraclitus, to the grove in which we are sitting, to the adventure in cosmic landscape art that we have just experienced, and to his words of wisdom and encouragement that made it possible.

Although the site at Atlanta is buried in trees, the effect upon the mind of the juxtaposition in the landscape of objects of various kinds was disturbing. The first Heraclitian thought to present itself was paramount: 'The unconscious harmonises the conscious'. Such a statement seems not to have been made again until Jung. There followed: 'Unity is only possible if there are opposites'. But how, for example, can this come about when the neo-Italian Renaissance mansion and the great new museum now being built are so obviously antagonistic? Then came the hidden clue, concealed in the famous words: 'All things are in flux'. Was it possible for the first time in the history of environment to create consciously a subconscious emotional force that would itself be more lasting in the subconscious than would static architecture? Could the Way be more significant than the Stops? Could it become a metaphysical journey in time and space, whose 'Beginnings and ends are shared in the circumference of a circle'? We have ourselves returned to where we began. We have retained Plato's great dictum that all art must be in correspondence with the cosmos; nor have we forgotten that the most stable civilisation in history, Egypt, waits upon a river into which you cannot step twice.

But enough of these ruminations. Our companion is becoming restless to leave, to go in search of myself. And so must we.

AN ITALIAN STUDY 1923-1925

CONTENTS

INTRODUCTION

This assessment is primarily that of architectural draughtsmanship as an interpretation of history. Since the original *Italian Gardens of the Renaissance* was published there have been deeper studies of history and wider and better photography but, by common consent, the series of drawings by my co-author, Jock Shepherd, has never been surpassed. This study describes and evaluates the various phases of its making: 1) choice of subject of study, 2) method of survey, 3) drawing technique, 4) drawings as the interpretation of history, 5) the reproduction of the Italian garden.

Choice of Subject of Study

The following engaging paragraph appeared in the Foreword to the 1986 facsimile edition of *Italian Gardens of the Renaissance* (Academy Edition).

> At the latter end of July 1923 two fifth year students of the Architectural Association in London invited their year-master (L.H. Bucknall, to whom the book was to be dedicated) to tea at the adjoining Plane Tree restaurant in Great Russell Street. The purpose was to seek advice for some specialist study as an academic anchor to a year's tour of Europe. Should it be cathedrals, piazzas, or what? The year master suggested over buttered scones that an architectural appraisal of Italian gardens might be fruitful, for no surveys had been made since the somewhat crude drawings of the French architects Percier and Fontaine a hundred years previously. The proposal was adopted. The students, armed with drawing board, paper, instruments and camera, set forth early in September.
>
> They travelled slowly through France on their way to Venice and thence to their first garden, the Villa Dona dalle Rose, Valzanzibio. Here, in an off-season spa hotel, the survey made during the day was drawn on paper; the sheer beauty of the plan revealed; and the making of a book, as a contribution to knowledge, inevitable.

The choice of individual gardens was made mainly from information in England. Like most fifth-year students we were acutely discriminating, at first choosing only purist examples prior to 1600 A.D. The later publication was in fact called *Italian Gardens of the Renaissance,* a title that covered only half the contents. Though the Dona dalle Rose opened up a wider vision, we still rejected the Villa d'Este at Tivoli as being vulgar, and the lovely Isola Bella on Lake Maggiore as being decadent. Este was copied later in England from an inaccurate plan; Isola Bella emerged with graceful apologies in the third edition.

Method of Survey

The majority of the surveys were original; those that existed were checked and redrawn. While Shepherd photographed, I would do the work on the ground. As students we had been taught the orthodox method of survey with precision instruments, and this took time. In architecture exactness is essential; in landscape it is not always required. Confronted with the vast area of the Villa

Dona dalle Rose, with only one day available, it was clear that orthodox methods were impossible. The traditional way of the layman was adopted: survey by pacing. We were in good company for John Evelyn records that he had so paced the Villa Valmarana some 250 years previously. Error of detail pacing within overall known dimensions (as in Ordnance Survey) need not exceed 5 per cent.

By the time we were half way through our programme I found that I could walk on to a site, take stock and then make a preparatory diagram (to which measurements would be added) that was a fair replica of the final plan when drawn out.

Measurement of landscape survey by pacing has two qualities that architecture has not. Walking is tactile. During the process and while you are counting, you are subconsciously absorbing the tactile qualities around you: the material you tread, the foliage you touch, as well as the smells, the sound of wind and water and birds, and not infrequently what you can taste. The other quality is that while in architecture you measure and put on to paper what is visible and static, this is not so in landscape. The eye may comprehend the visible contents of a site and even imagine the seasonable changes but it requires the subconscious faculty to comprehend the plan, which is abstract and invisible.

The lasting value to myself of such a year of survey has been the ability to relate drawing board unusually closely to site.

Drawing Technique

The surveys were drawn as usual, first in pencil with shadows added at 45 per cent, length equalling height, and fixed by rubbed-down Indian ink. Jock Shepherd, who now took over, based his tones on those of the French designer, Gromort. The first drawing, that of the Dona dalle Rose, was a success. The tone values and shadows together caused sparkle and luminosity. Be not deceived by their apparent simplicity. Some eight years later, while I was preparing my own study of Austrian Baroque gardens, I was determined in this comparative volume to repeat the Shepherd luminous tone values. The subject was the gardens of Schönbrunn. I spent a week in a charming hostelry in Salzburg trying out sheet after sheet of experiments. I failed miserably, tore up the drawings, put them down the loo, pulled the plug and decided there and then I could never be anything but a mediocre draughtsman (a view I maintained without argument for fifty years). The drawings of the Austrian gardens were later made in line by Alison, Jock Shepherd's wife.

The perspective sketches in *Italian Gardens of the Renaissance* that introduce many of the villas were made by Shepherd later in England, free-hand from memory and at the request of the publishers. The script lettering was added by a fellow student more accomplished than ourselves in calligraphy.

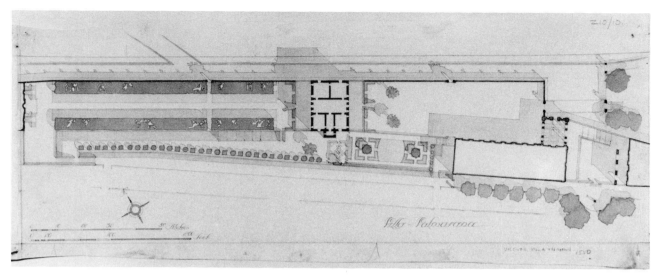

Plan of Villa Valmarana; drawing technique by J.C. Shepherd

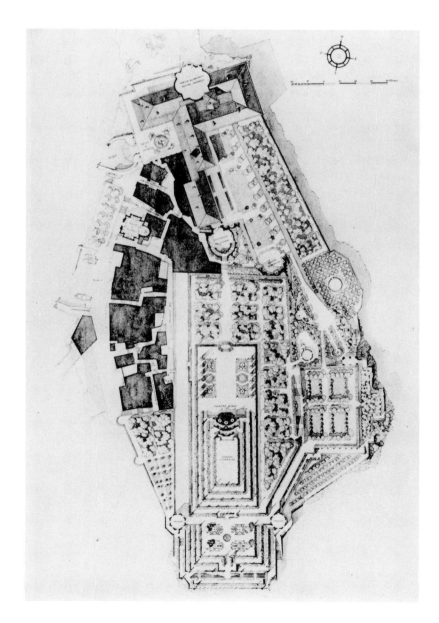

Gromort's drawing of Isola Bella from Jardins d'Italie, *source of drawing technique by J.C. Shepherd*

Drawings as the Interpretation of History

The philosophy of the drawings goes back beyond Gromort to the classics, to plates such as that of the Roman capital illustrated on page 13. When congratulated on the excellence of his own drawings, Shepherd would deny that the art was his: it was not, it was that of the gardens themselves. The artist has subdued both his own ego and anything ephemeral (such as trees, which are drawn abstract) for one purpose only: to emphasise form. It is pure form reflected in drawing that explains why such disparate subjects as Bramante's Belvedere Court of about 1500 A.D. can be reconciled with the Villa Rasponi c.1575 A.D. and the Villa Carlotta c.1750 A.D. (overleaf).

For *form,* abstract and invisible, revealed, explored and developed by the Greeks, is the Jungian archetype of all classical art, irrespective of time, place and individual emotions. What *is* significant form, as it is sometimes called? We know it to be based on proportion; but what is proportion and why should humans respond to it and feel calmed and enriched? We recognise the standard classical proportions like the mathematical rectangles, the golden section, the fundamental proportions of Plato, but do these cover the infinity of shapes which we know, enjoy and find unaccountable — not only the western but those of Islam and China?

The sense of proportion as expressed through geometry is clearly a projection of the human mind searching for an order that does not exist in the laws of nature. Let us, as did Goethe when proposing a theory of the Pyramids and the cosmos, hazard a guess that all (yes, *all*) agreeable geometric proportion from the smallest rounded moulding to the monumental is based on its relation to that universal mythical form, the circle, the mother of geometry.

The Reproduction of the Italian Garden in the Modern World

There were two reasons why it was hoped that these purist drawings would help expose false images of the Italian garden that were proliferating (and continue to proliferate) throughout the western world.

Firstly, photography alone cannot capture the feeling of a garden. It is concerned with a single viewpoint, or a series of single viewpoints, which are usually chosen on merit as illustrations rather than information. The viewpoint cannot convey the plan, the abstract form that masterminds all its seductive detail.

Secondly, unless revivified by a skilled designer, the copy cannot fail to be lifeless. The two forces of *classicism* and *romanticism* can be likened to underground rivers watering the soils and seeds on their way to infinity. The seeds break surface and flower. Whosoever takes cuttings and plants downstream will find that his beautiful flowers will wither away, being rootless.

In order to appreciate the emotional depths of classicism that gave rise to the greatest garden art the world has known, let us apply another simile for the

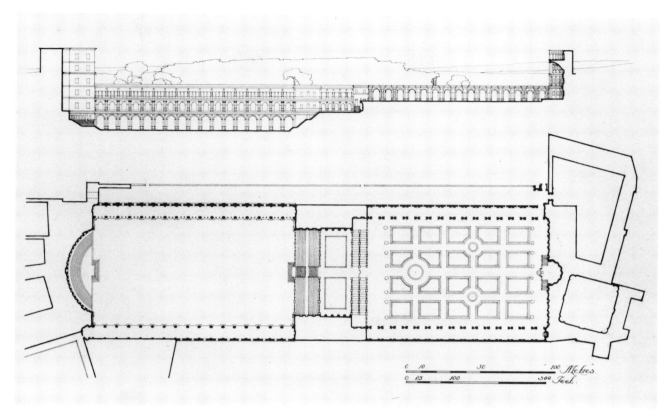

Belvedere Court of the Vatican by Bramante

Elevation of Villa Rasponi

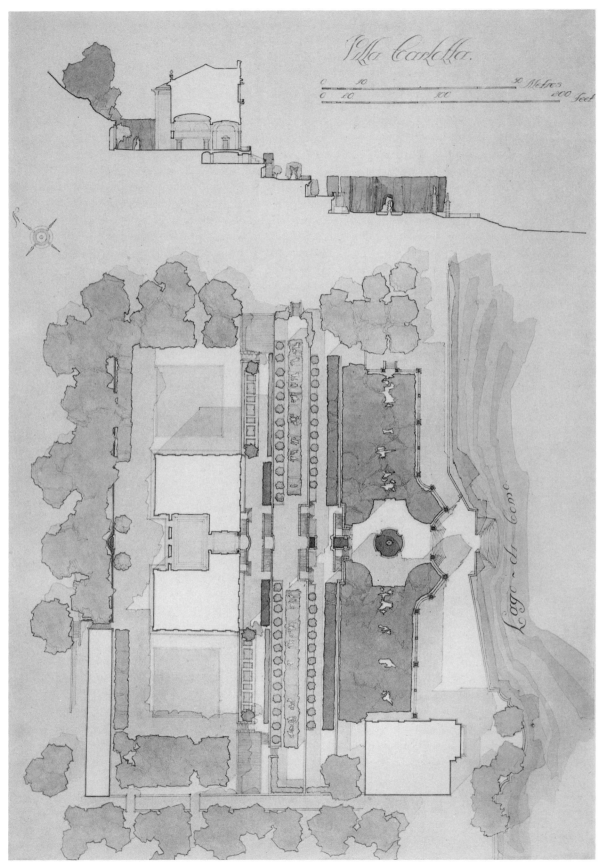

Villa Carlotta, Lake Como

three interlocking periods that have been designated in art: the Renaissance c.1400-1600, Mannerism c.1550-1650 and Baroque c.1600-1750.

The *Renaissance:* Imagine yourself in a glass box, curtained all round but not on top. Stirrings within you cause you to pull aside the curtain. A scene of unimaginable beauty is revealed. You now accept your containment happily enough for the new light discovers ancient manuscripts with a recipe as to how you can refashion the interior of the box to equate it with the lovely newly-revealed exterior. You follow instructions and comes the climax when heaven itself seems by you to have been brought to earth.

Mannerism: The cement that binds the box disintegrates. You smash the glass and feel for the first time ever, as a garden designer, the breath of freedom on your cheeks.

Baroque: Collective order is once more restored, your mind has been recaptured and put into a spectacular open prison. In due course you will again break free to travel unguided into the unknown.

Towards a Landscape of Humanism

This is primarily a statement of classical values. If we liken our present civilisation to a ship voyaging in unchartered and dangerous seas, with no knowledge of where we are going and, indeed, why — then it is critical. Our present ship is built of the tested materials of classicism and these we should be unwise to discard until we are certain that those of a new structure are stronger and more appropriate. But this does not apply to the contents of the ship and as furnishings we can dredge things out of the deep that we had never dreamed existed. *(The Guelph Lectures on Landscape Design)*

THE RENAISSANCE c.1400-1600

Expression: The eye that had previously looked inward upon an external world, now looked outwards to see the physical world and to find it good; Petrarch is said to have been the first western man to climb a mountain for the sake of the view. The change was one from symbolism to worldliness. To enhance these newly found pleasures, the house extended itself into the open air, creating what were defined spaces whose links were as important as were the internal doorways between salons. Views of the countryside were part of the design, rather in the manner of the classic frescoed wall; it was not until later that garden and landscape were physically more closely integrated. The fundamental purpose was to create shapes that responded to the intellectual mind searching for order, tranquillity and stimulus, giving dignity and status to the human himself. In principle, the sites overlooked the mother city from adjoining slopes or hillsides. The Florentine villa remained domestic, in spirit associated with its rural surroundings. The Roman villa was almost solely humanistic and heroic, the purpose being to reincarnate the spirit and grandeur of antiquity.

Villa Lante, Vignola's sublime landscape design. (Photograph Susan Jellicoe)

Landscape: The garden was made for man and dignified him. The proportions gave him peace: the form was therefore crucial. The interior of the house thrust itself outwards, levelled to the rising or falling site, the shapes made more by intuition than by mathematical calculation. The sites were usually on hillsides, because of view and climate; the descending terraces were carved out of the ground and harmonious with it; the long shapes were genial to contemplative perambulation. The contents were basically evergreens, stone and water — materials that were permanent rather than ephemeral. They included box parterres, clipped hedges, the dark cypress and groves of ilex; sculpture, stairways, pergolas and arbours; water in repose and in fountains. Flowers played little part. The architectural details were tactile and friendly through the emotional curves of mouldings, nosings, balusters. The wide versatility of design, especially in Tuscany, was caused by the endless combinations possible between the personality of the owner, of the architect and of the site. Vignola (1507-73) lifted landscape design into the sublime at the Villa Lante, subordinating architecture to an ancient and universal idea of cosmology. *(The Landscape of Man)*

Villa Medici, Fiesole; the Renaissance villa within its rural surroundings.
(Photograph Susan Jellicoe)

Perspective sketch

Villa Medici, Fiesole
(1458-61. Architect Michelozzo Michelozzi)

Florentine Humanism was an intellectual awakening that looked to Greece and Rome rather than to the Church for authority. Lorenzo de' Medici and his circle saw themselves as the heirs of the Platonic Academy and tried to recreate for themselves the cultured life about which they read in Horace and Pliny. At the same time, they could not at once rid themselves of the conventions of the Middle Ages. The early Medici Villa by Michelozzo Michelozzi at Cafaggiolo (1451) is still essentially a medieval fortified house with compartmented garden. A few years later, however, at the Villa Medici at Fiesole, the same architect created the first true Renaissance villa. The idea was similar to that of the Generalife at Granada, made by the Moors some century and a half previously. The house is projected along the hillside into the open air. The gardens are still formal and regular but the surrounding countryside has been brought into the design. The upper terrace, artificially formed by a huge retaining wall, looks out over Florence. Below lies a traditional pergola. No longer in any way symbolic, the garden has become a setting for pleasure and philosophical debate. *(The Landscape of Man)*

Colour plate page 114

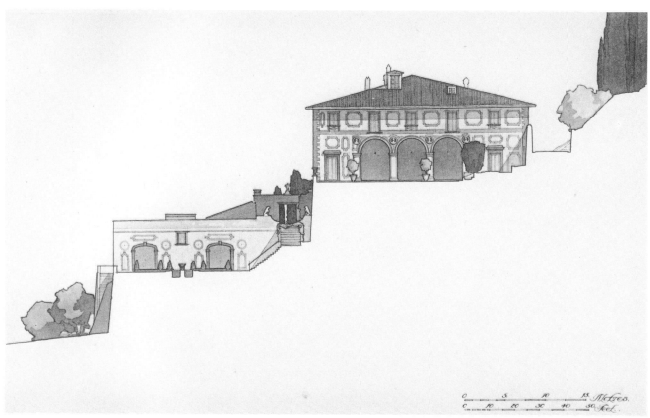

Section

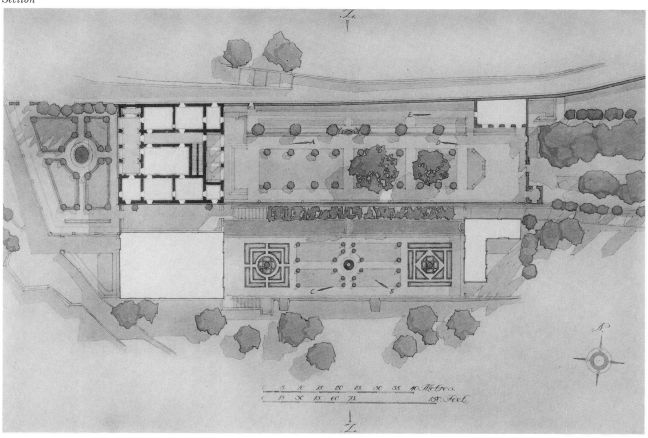

Plan

continued

Five views of the Villa Medici, Fiesole

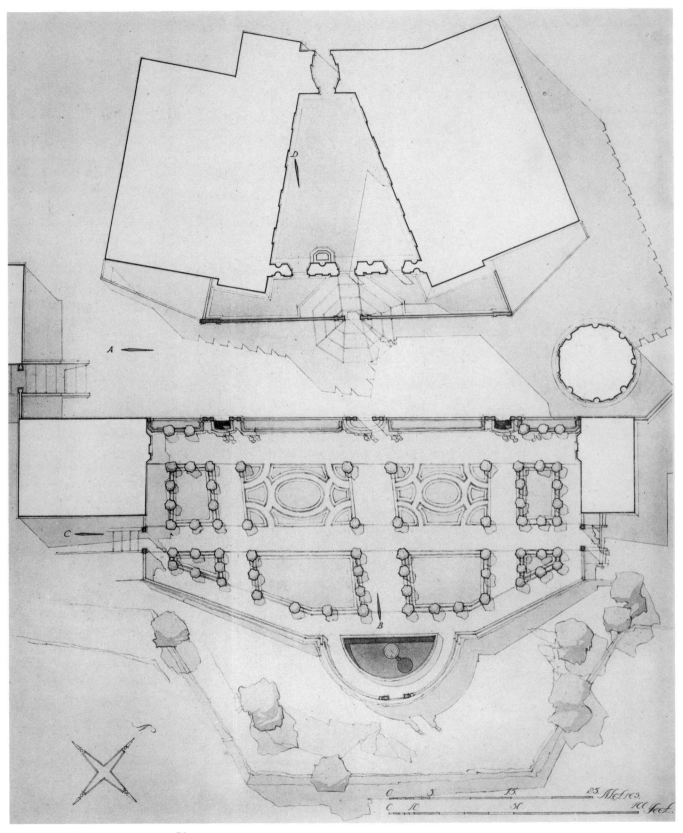

Plan

Villa Celsa, near Siena
(Early 16th century. Attributed to Peruzzi)

The gardens of Baldassare Peruzzi, the famous Sienese architect who lived from 1481 to 1537, have proved to be almost as ephemeral as those described by Girolamo Firenzuola. Though two gardens near Siena — Vicobello and Celsa — are attributed to him, both have subsequently been so altered that today neither of them resembles his garden design preserved in the Uffizi except in the simplicity of their basic plans. The geometrical parterres and paths shaded by what the Italians call a 'berso' — the vaulted trellis or pleached alley known as a cradle or 'berceau' in French — have disappeared.

At Celsa, however, there is definite evidence that they once existed which, in view of Peruzzi's authorship of the near-by circular chapel, renders it likely that the garden was also originally designed by him. A drawing preserved in the Castle of Celsa shows the little garden, with the marvellous view, that lies in front of it, laid out with berso-covered paths and a circular fountain placed in the curve of the wall on the far side. Probably about the middle of the seventeenth century, while still preserving its original ground plan, this garden was transformed by the addition of imposing gateways and the creation of a semicircular pool on the site of the old fountain. These changes formed part of an ambitious project for the conversion of the medieval castle into an elaborate villa, of which a drawing also exists in the castle.

The only parts of the project that were put into effect, however, were the erection of the screen that links the two wings of the castle and the additions to the garden. The elaborate broderies shown in the project were apparently never planted in the parterres, as when Shepherd and Jellicoe drew a plan of the garden in 1925 these still retained their old geometrical layout which was very similar to those of Peruzzi's garden plan in the Uffizi. (*Italian Gardens*)

continued

Villa Celsa, near Siena

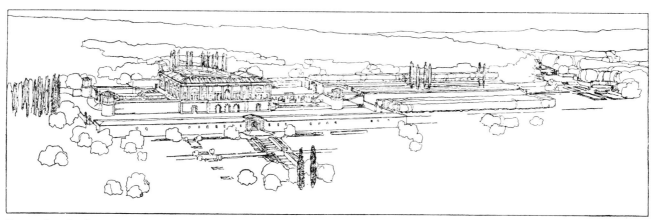

Perspective sketch

Villa Madama, Rome
(Early 16th century)

It was a Tuscan, Cardinal Giulio de' Medici, who built the first Renaissance villa outside the walls of Rome. Its site on the slopes of Monte Mario overlooking the city may well have reminded a Medici of his family's famous Fiesole villa, while the splendour of the view and the countrified freshness of the surroundings would have held an instant appeal for a man reared in the Florentine humanist tradition. But here all resemblance with a Tuscan country house practically ceased as the Villa Madama, as it has been known for centuries owing to the subsequent ownership of Margaret of Austria, was entirely Roman in spirit and monumental grandeur.

The plan is one of the most perfect examples of the interpenetration of house and garden in existence, rivalling even the pavilions of Hadrian's villa in this respect, and its influence on Italian garden design was to be second only to that of Bramante. But this magnificent layout was destined never to be completed.
(Italian Gardens)

continued

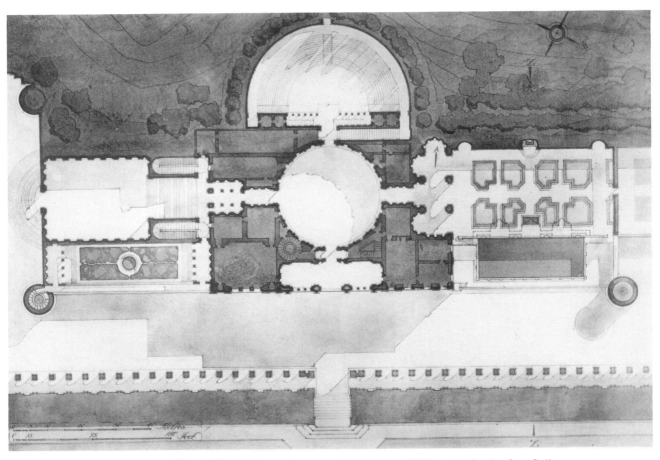

Plan, Villa Madama, from an original in the Uffizi collection by San Gallo

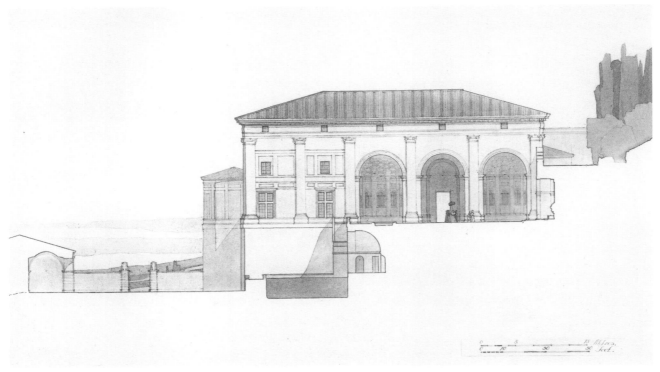

Section, Villa Madama, restoration from existing building in comparison with the plan

Villa Madama, Rome

Perspective sketch

Boboli Gardens, Florence
(c. 1550. Architects Tribolo and Buontalenti)

The Boboli gardens are a return to the box with the curtains closed (page 69), but the form within the box is new. Although the gardens have seen many changes, the form itself is basically 1550, made mainly from the quarry that provided stone for the Pitti Palace. There is the feeling of Baroque in the sequence of shapes carved out of woodlands and clearly, too, of the future work of Le Nôtre in France, with his concept of the expansion of space as it recedes from the palace.

A cross avenue leads to the Isolotto (1618), an island fantasy inspired by the Maritime Theatre in Hadrian's Villa. At the summit, on Michaelangelo's ramparts of Florence, is the Giardino del Cavalieri (17th century), a *giardino segreto* with the only window on the outer world.

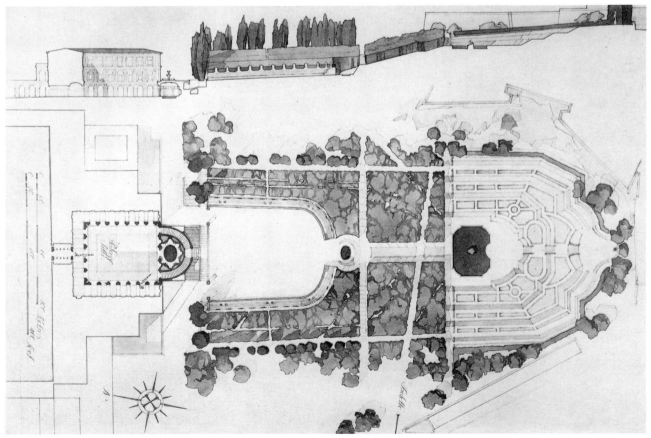

Plan

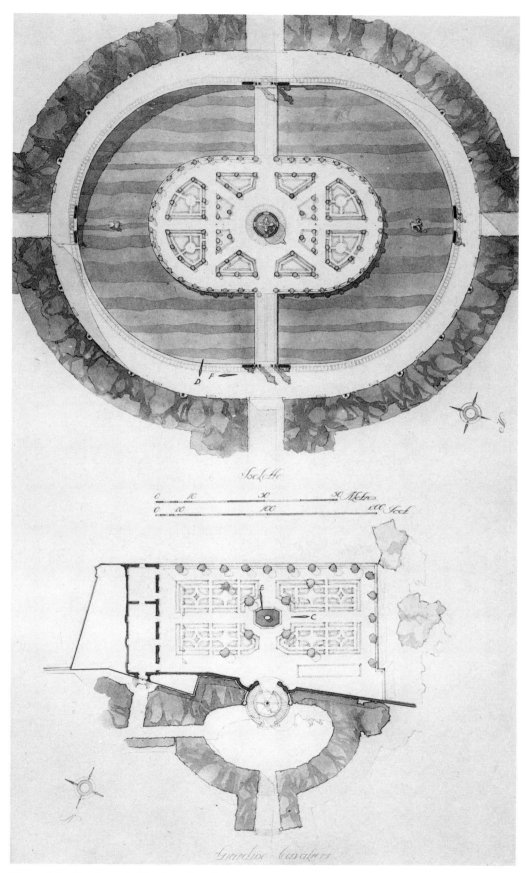

Isolotto

Giardino Cavalieri

Plans of the Isolotto and Giardino Cavalieri

continued

Six views of the Boboli Gardens, Florence

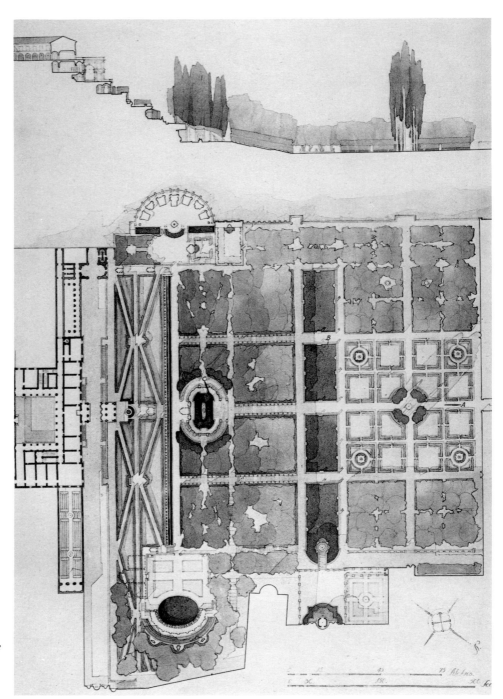

Plan. The central axis is askew; the drawing was made from an earlier plan which we unwisely assumed to be correct

Villa d'Este Tivoli
(1550. Architect Pirro Ligorio)

The Villa d'Este at Tivoli, shown in the contemporary print by Etienne du Perac, is the most spectacular and sumptuous of the gardens of the High Roman Renaissance. Made in 1550 by Pirro Ligorio, the conception is based on antique Roman — not only the nearby Hadrian's Villa (from which sculpture was taken) but also Ligorio's own re-creation of the classical Temple of Fortune at Praeneste. The plan is accomplished, the modelling on the steep hillside firm, the detail robust and the transition between gardens and landscape clearly defined; over all is the sense of Roman domination of

landscape. The central vista looks north-west across the Tiber to the Sabatina Mountains. The triumphal arch that terminates the upper terrace looks towards Rome. Below this is the Rometta, or 'little Rome', with its models of antiquity. The gardens — now shady with cypress trees — everywhere echo to the sound of water, diverted through a conduit from the river Aniene and spread lavishly and musically through the garden: the water organ with its reflecting fish pools, the terrace of a hundred fountains and through many other equally refreshing devices. *(The Landscape of Man)*

Plan

Villa Pia, Vatican Gardens
(1560. Architect Pirro Ligorio)

Designed ten years later by the architect of the Villa d'Este, the Villa Pia is complementary to it in idea as well as form. The summer retreat of Pope Pius IV in the Vatican gardens, it is a gem of classical open space design and a folly that is a worthy companion to Vignola's Casino at Caprarola.

Plan

Villa Piccolomini, Frascati
(c.1560. Architect unknown. Partially destroyed in the Second World War)

After Bramante's Belvedere Court of the Vatican, this was perhaps the finest 'closed box' garden in Renaissance Italy, being an extension of the interior of the villa to become a magnificent outdoor salon with its carpet of parterre. A reconstruction forms the basis of the Italian Renaissance garden for the Moody Historical Gardens at Galveston, Texas, published in *The Landscape of Civilisation*.

It has been recorded that on approaching the owners who were sitting in the garden, we were refused entry. While Jock Shepherd argued the point, I put in some crucial pacings. With the aid of a map for overall dimensions and public photographs by Alinari, we reconstructed the design as shown.

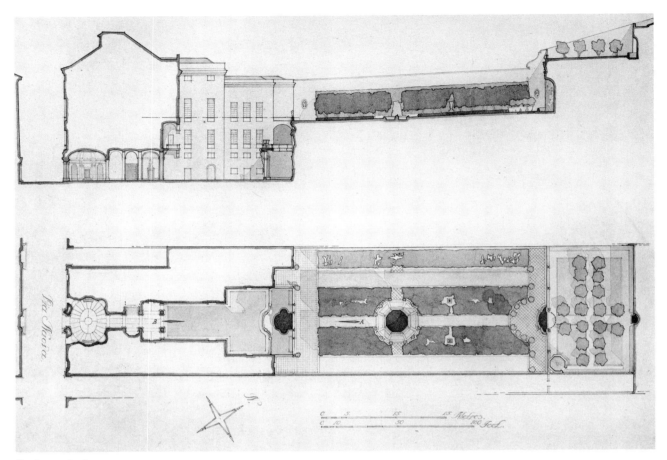

Section and plan

Palazzo Podesta, Genoa
(1563. Architect Castello Bergamesco. Fountain added late 17th century by Parodi)

The Palazzo Podesta was designed in 1563 for Niccolo Lomellini by Giovanni Battista Castello (Il Bergamesco); fountains were added by Filippo Parodi c.1700. The street of palaces (the Strada Nuova, now Via Garibaldi) had been laid out in 1550, presumably by Galeazzo Alessi. The street is a canyon, with openings whose average height is about two and a half times the width. Of the palaces on the north side of the Strada Nuova, laid out from 1550, which abut a steep hillside, the Podesta is the only one with its fine Baroque garden still intact. The width of the site is about 25 metres and the depth about 120 metres of which over a third is taken up by the mansion. From the claustrophobic street a vista leads through the entrance hall and courtyard to a rococo fountain above which terraces are ingeniously arranged to connect with the first and second floors of the palazzo, but the real charm lies in the creation of imaginative space in a confined area. As the vista recedes, the detail tends to be reduced in scale, and while the main terrace is visible in its entirety from the upper floors, the final garden of orange trees can be seen only suggestively and remotely. This vertical design in a vertical dimension is completed by a 16 metre high tower to view the sea beyond the roofs. *(Oxford Companion to Gardens)*

We were given no more nor less than twenty minutes for the survey and photography.

Elevation

Villa Bombicci near Florence
(c.1560. Attributed to Santi di Tito and associated with Michelangelo)

The garden layout is in keeping with the severe grandeur of the house, and its main features are the magnificent cypress avenue that provides a suitably dignified approach to the house and the spacious terrace, with its all-embracing view, that lies before it. *(Italian Gardens)*

Plan

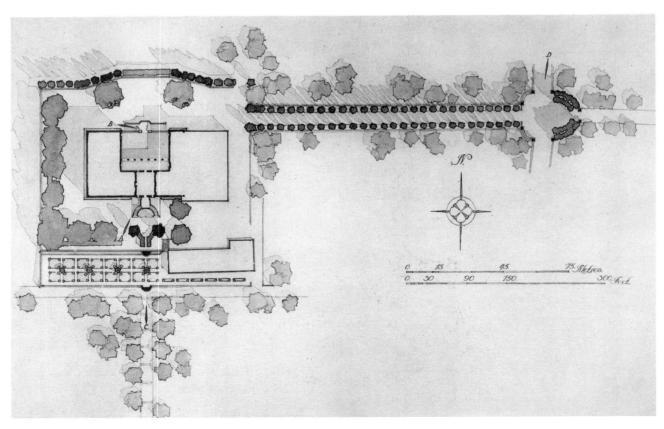

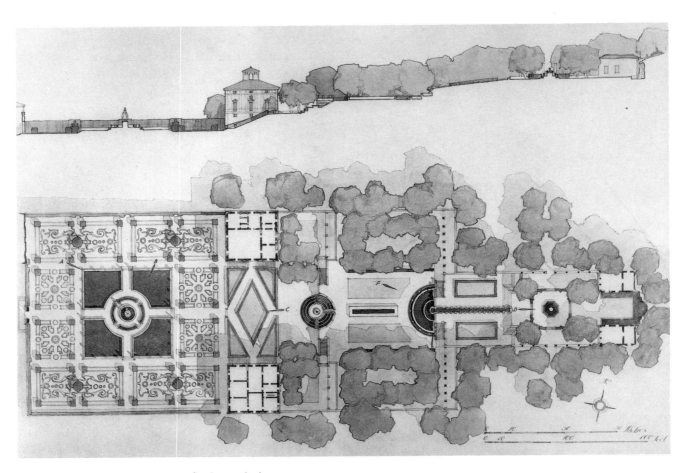

Section and plan

Villa Lantè, Bagnaia
(Begun 1564, completed 1573. Architect Vignola)

Vignola is generally accepted as the greatest garden architect (not landscape designer) the world has known and the Villa Lante the greatest of his works. The conception is linked with the neighbouring Palazzo Farnese at Caprarola and subsequently with the casino hidden in its park (pages 100-103). In 1547 Vignola had been commissioned to build the mighty Farnese Palace on existing fortress foundations. The shape was a pentagon with a central circular court. The gardens that fashion demanded presented a problem. The form must be powerful enough to be a significant projection of the odd shape. He chose the firmest shape known to man, the square.

We can now imagine him fascinated by a shape not particularly significant in western civilisation but profoundly so throughout the world elsewhere as the earthly counterpart of the heavenly circle.

The Lante gardens themselves were begun in 1564. Vignola is now preoccupied with the square; to give it significance he divided the building into two parts, material objects in attendance upon a metaphysical idea that may have been inspired by Perugino's *Christ giving the keys to St. Peter*. The revolutionary concept of a paramount landscape has arrived.

Colour plates page 115

continued

Four views of Villa Lante, Bagnaia

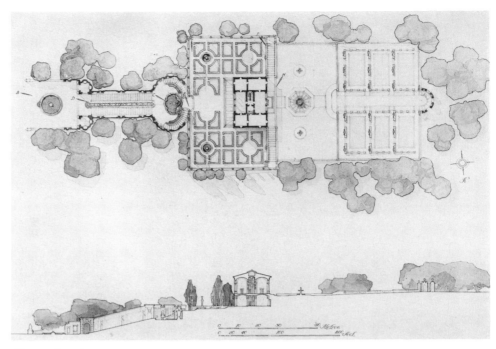

Plan and section

The Casino, Palazzo Farnese, Caprarola
(Completed 1687. Architect Vignola)

During the making of the most overwhelming villa in Italy, the owner, Cardinal Alexander Farnese, would have been aware of the Villa Pia in the Vatican gardens and appreciated the idea of escape from reality. At some unknown date he commissioned Vignola for a similar but more majestic folly hidden in the park. Vignola died in 1573, but not before he had left designs for a secret retreat whose sense of form (traceable back to the receding scale of his Villa Papa Julio, 1550), of mythology, and of the pure fun of life, are with us today.

Elevation of Casino, Palazzo Farnese

Palazzo Farnese

The Casino, Palazzo Farnese

continued

Six views of the Casino, Palazzo Farnese, Caprarola

Villa Bernadini, Saltocchio, Lucca
(c.1590)

The gardens are a transition between the High Renaissance and Baroque. The two enclosures are finite, but within the larger there is the imaginative invention of the decorative woodland bosco, later to be developed in France.

The open space between villa and bosco is about 15 metres short of that shown in the plan. The mistake was discovered after the drawing had been completed and inked in late at night in the hotel in Lucca. I was too tired to redraw it.

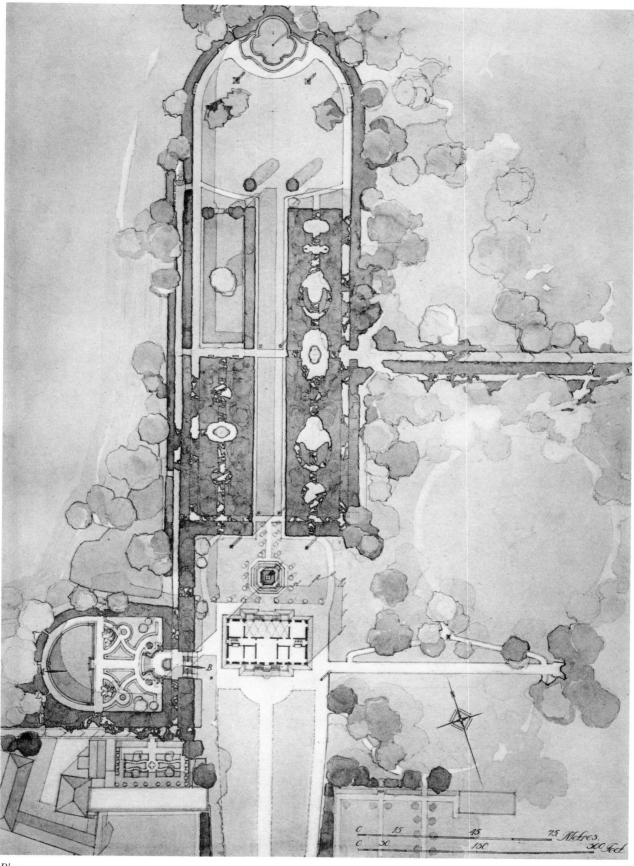

Plan

C   15   45   75 *Metres.*

C   30   150   300 *Feet.*

105

Perspective sketch Villa La Pietra

Villa Poggio Torselli, near Florence
Villa La Pietra, near Florence
(17th century. Probably by the same architect)

These two grand villas in the country on either side of Florence are examples of the pure Renaissance projected into a later age. The recipe was standard and traditional: the authoritarian cypress avenue across the farmlands to the villa with its cluster of gardens, sometimes (as at Poggio Torselli) in the sole form of a framed view terrace.

Colour plate Villa La Pietra page 114

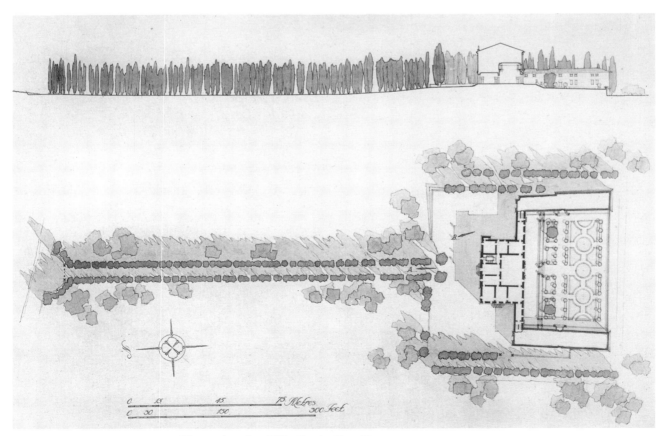

Plan and section Villa Poggio Torselli

Top and above: Villa Poggio Torselli

continued

Villa La Pietra, near Florence

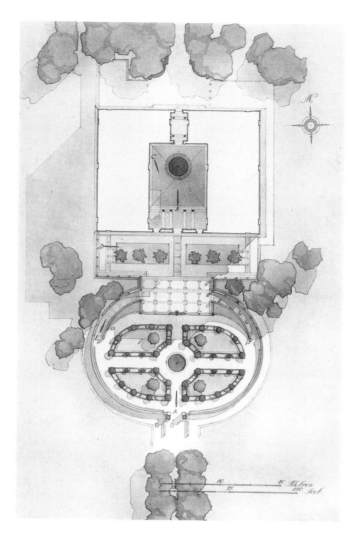

Plan

Villa Palmieri, Florence
(1690)

One cannot but feel that its competent design made in the form of the High Renaissance, is less inspired than the earlier garden it replaced. Although Boccaccio's work painting a picture of gay Neapolitan life, *Visione Amorosa,* was probably begun in Naples it was completed in Florence about 1345, three years before he began his masterpiece, *The Decameron,* whose setting was the garden of the Villa Palmieri, which affords us the most vivid portrayal of *villeggiatura* life in a Tuscan villa. The garden of the Villa Palmieri today dates only from the seventeenth century, but in Boccaccio's time it was evidently still predominantly medieval in character, with the familiar layout of a fountain standing in the midst of a flower-starred lawn and vine pergolas and shaded walks. In size, however, it seems to have been bigger than most medieval gardens and its planting more elaborate; the walks were bordered not only by roses but also by citrus trees and jasmine. In this sylvan setting, peopled also by rabbits and kids, the young protagonists of *The Decameron* crowned each other with flowers and sang and danced in the morning, dined by the fountain, rested in the shade playing chess and reading *Lives of the Romans* in the afternoon, and in the evening gathered in the meadow to tell their tales. *(Italian Gardens)*

continued

Five views of Villa Palmieri, Florence

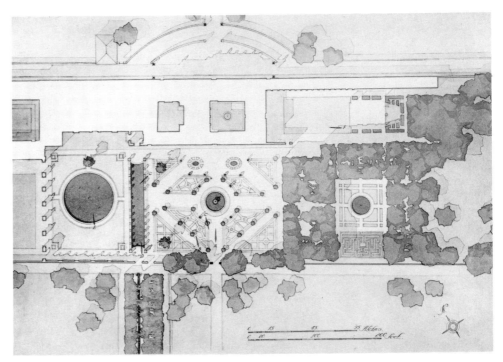

Plan

Villa Corsi Salviati, Sesto
(1502-1637; 1660-1738)

These gardens in the flat Arno valley are a continuum of the Florentine tradition of geometrical enclosures gradually developing into an enjoyable sequence of shapes. Ultimately the dullness of site provoked a Baroque outburst of silhouette.

The survey was followed with intense interest by the owner, the Marchese Giulio Guiccardini Corsi Salviati, who asked and received a copy of the final rendered drawing. He opened many doors for us throughout Italy and we remained in contact until the Second World War.

Villa Medici, Fiesole, overlooking Florence from a typical Renaissance hillside site

Villa La Pietra, Florence; pure Renaissance projected into a later age

Villa Lante, Bagnaia, the rill

Fountain, Villa Lante. Villa Lante's garden is considered the greatest work of the great Renaissance garden architect Vignola

115

MANNERISM c.1550-1650

After the sack of Rome by the Spaniards in 1527 the power of the church over the collective mind disintegrated. The golden age of classicism, its outward expression and which brooked no breach of the rules, now showed ominous cracks. Two of these were momentous in the history of garden art: eccentricity and individuality.

Eccentricity was anti-classicism. It created such revolutionary objects as the huge giant and pre-Baroque descending pools at the Villa Medici, Pratolino, near Florence. In Florence itself the Ammanati grotto in the Boboli Gardens points the way to modern surrealism with all its significance. At Bomarzo in the vicinity of the classical masterpiece, the Villa Lante, an owner rebellious of society as a whole, created a park of monsters who emerged from the underworld to destroy civilisation and, if need be, to swallow it whole. The authors of *Italian Gardens of the Renaissance* clearly did not feel that such oddities came within their terms of reference; but individuality did. Individuality created two novel ideas: that the owner acquired the garden he wanted and not what the rules dictated; and that the garden broke free from its subservience to the house. The landscape designer emerged in his own right to handle both these matters.

Left and above: The Ammanati grotto in the Boboli Gardens, Florence, characteristic of the Mannerist escape from reality to individuality

Villa Gamberaia, Settignano, a Mannerist garden with a place for every mood

Villa Gamberaia, Settignano

Villa Marlia, Lucca

Villa Marlia, Lucca; the garden ranges from parterre to Baroque fantasy giants

Above and right: Villa Garzoni, Collodi, with characteristic Baroque statuary

Villa Capponi, Arcetri
(c.1574; modern lower terrace parterre)

The lane that leads out of Florence to Arcetri is bordered on either side by villas built directly on to the road. Though dull walls usually hide the gardens, those of the Villa Capponi are frankly delighting in what they conceal. Behind them lies a garden almost perfect for a small villa just outside the city. The long lawn, calm and restful, soothes the uneven lines of the building: but once beyond the house, the garden bursts into a box of pleasaunce and terraces. The terraces follow a fall in the ground, and from the breezy openness of the lawn, steps descend into the seclusion of two secret gardens, sinking into the olive trees around. Here parterre, lemon trees, bushes and pool are framed in by wall tops so bubbling with fun that they chase away the cares of all who come.
(Italian Gardens of the Renaissance)

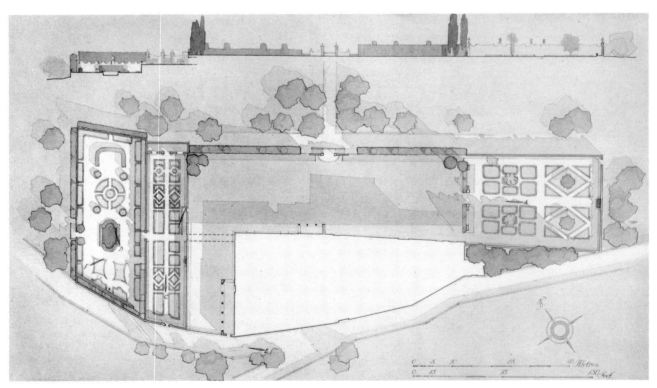

Section and plan

continued

Villa Capponi, Arcetri

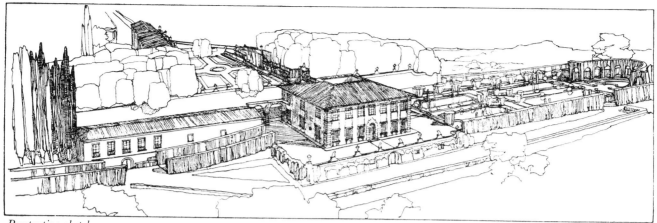

Perspective sketch

Villa Gamberaia, Settignano
(c.1610; water garden a modern adaptation from 17th century parterre)

The house of the Villa Gamberaia, now mellowed to a soft ivory colour and perfectly embodying the Tuscan ideal of restraint and proportion, is the centre of a garden that varies with every aspect: playful where the pools and the box hedges and singing frogs lie basking in the sun; stately where the bowling alley sweeps into the dark grandeur of cypresses; and simple where the olive valley runs down to Florence. There is a place for every mood. Hamlet will find an answering chord in the twilight of the bosco, mysterious, elusive, fantastic with the shapes of ilex; the joker can go and joke among the water steps and grotto; and the two can agree to differ in the most delightful of lemon gardens. As one walks from place to place in this garden of less than three acres, there seems to be something about it more Italian than the Italians themselves. That character has been understood and provided for with an intuition of real sympathy. (*Italian Gardens of the Renaissance*)

Colour plates page 118

continued

Villa Gamberaia, Settignano

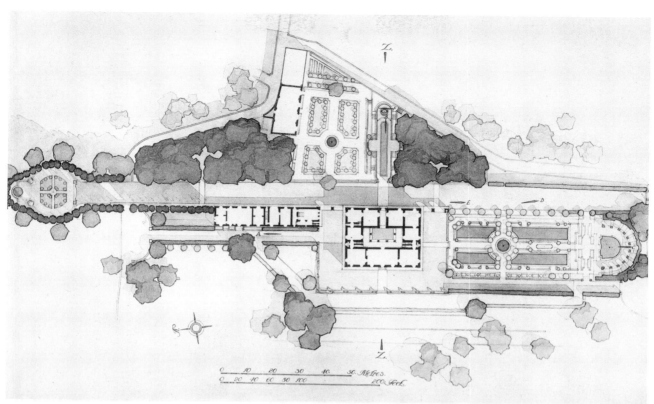

Plan Villa Gamberaia

Section and elevation Villa Gamberaia

Villa Garzoni, Collodi. It was on the creation of imaginative space and movement that Baroque art depended. (Photograph Susan Jellicoe)

BAROQUE c.1600-1750

Astronomical discoveries, combined with the questioning of religious dogma had thrown doubt upon the very foundations of the existing order and beliefs. Individual and thoughtful man found himself groping for something beyond his understanding; common people as a whole still remained intensely religious and it was this passionate emotion that the Counter Reformation was determined to capture and exploit, through art as well as teaching. The assault was led by the Jesuits, whose understanding of the conflict in the human mind was acute. They conceded that man might have an influence upon the shaping of his own destiny — a fundamental break with medieval theology. They accepted the change in man's relation to the universe, and that all things were in flux; and set out in church architecture to create emotional environments that would answer subconscious yearnings and overcome all reason. From the staggering revolution in church design sprang a new conception of space that was to spread to all realms of art, especially of landscape design and town planning.

The second half of the sixteenth century was a transition from one philosophical concept to another: from the classical finite to the Baroque infinite. The expression of the finite is factual, that of infinity can only be imaginative. The mind and not the eye takes charge, and it was on the creation of imaginative space and movement that Baroque art depended. It was technically based on illusion and the newly found art of the theatre. In church interiors, the space volumes followed one another in progression, culminating in the great painted vision of the heavens that blasted away the confining ceiling. Architecturally the parts were in constant and imaginative movement, symbolised by curve chasing curve. Externally, and most notable in landscape design, an awareness that man was not only a part of a swirling complex that embraced rocks and water as well as the heavens, established the idea that an object was not an object in itself but related to others in an infinite chain. All these objects, and not man alone, now inspired his design. From rocks he finally created the abstract forms of the Trevi Fountain (1735), probably the most symbolic achievement of the age; from water and shells he created countless shifting abstract forms; from the movements of the sea he made the Salute Church in Venice; he joined heaven and earth with the water's reflecting mirror. The synthesis of the environment as a whole entity and as a part of infinity had now begun. (*The Landscape of Man*)

Perspective sketch

Villa Torlonia, Frascati
(1623. Architect Carlo Maderna)

The addition of the nave and west façade of St. Peter's that transformed Michelangelo's Greek cross into a Latin cross preoccupied Maderna for more than twenty years. The policy was theological rather than aesthetic and the extension inevitably spoiled the view of the dome from the approach; nevertheless, Maderna's design is a stupendous interior clearly inspired by Vignola's church of the Gesu. Bernini's piazza was not yet in being and Maderna must have revolved in his imagination what might be the future piazza and the realigned streets behind, to which his façade would be the climax. It would seem that the Villa Torlonia represents these ideas transferred to landscape.

The site, with its spectactular views over the Campagna, can be likened to that of a waterside city such as Lisbon, the design itself falling into three parts: the approaches, the town proper and the basilica. The monumental stairways of the approach indicate at once that the whole concept is an abstract, for these would enable to pass with dignity more than two thousand persons a minute — an unlikely number for Frascati but reasonable for the piazza of St. Peter's. The stairways, which were planned to triangulate the cascade, lead up to a promenade and thence into the green ilex gridiron of the streets. The streets then lead to a double square piazza, closed with a composition that might be an abstract of the façade, nave and dome of St. Peter's, a truly majestic fantasy of landscape.

The plan appears to make room for the house, itself unimportant; the whole of the terraces and flights of steps were moved past their relative positions to the garden above. This alteration could only have been made while the work was in progress. *(Italian Gardens of the Renaissance)*.

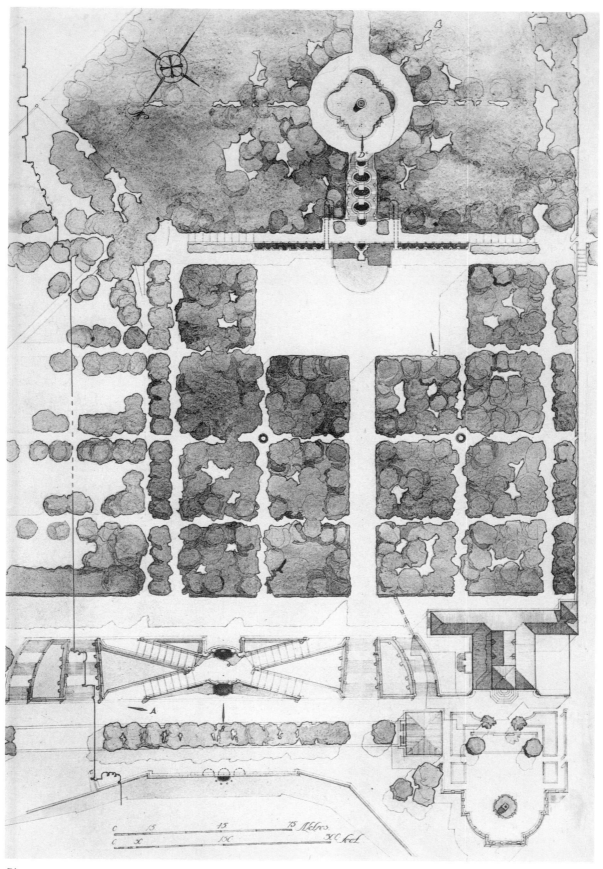

Plan

continued

Four views of Villa Torlonia, Frascati

continued

Elevation of cascade Villa Torlonia, Frascati

Perspective sketch

Villa Garzoni, Collodi
(Begun 1652)

Built on the foundations of a medieval castle, the villa itself stands on a hillside, concealing the village behind. The new garden is separated from the villa by a public road but has been swung in such a way that the lower parterre can be seen from the windows.

Although there is access at the high level, it is visually an independent landscape, owing as much to Roman as to Florentine influence. The lower parterre is furnished with twin circular pools and family heraldry in box and is outlined into curve and counter-curve with double scalloped hedges. From this level, three promenade terraces rise spectacularly against a background of trees, the uppermost terminating in a charming garden theatre. Axially in the centre, steps and stairways ascend to a great cascade (whose rocks are fashioned like an elongated giant) that parts the woods and disappears against a statue of Fame deep in the bosco at the summit. Beside this statue is the bath house thought to have been converted in the eighteenth century from a seventeenth century hermitage. The detail throughout the garden is somewhat crude, but this does not detract from the beauty of shape. Technically the gardens, fortunately still well preserved, are a box of Baroque optical tricks: the cascade, for instance, widens as it ascends, making it look more abrupt when seen from below and longer when seen from above. *(Oxford Companion to Gardens)*

Colour plates page 119

continued

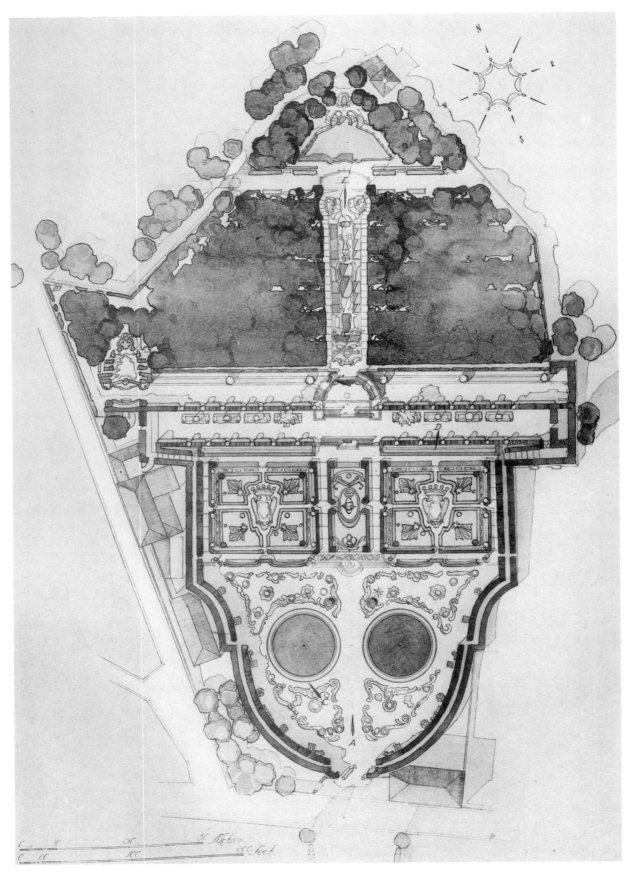

Plan Villa Garzoni

Villa Garzoni, Collodi

continued

Villa Garzoni, Collodi

Villa Marlia, Lucca
(Late 17th century)

The Villa Marlia was laid out in the late seventeenth century by the Orsetti family; from 1806 to 1814 it was the summer residence of Napoleon's sister, Elisa Baciocchi, who added neo-classical modifications and enlarged the garden. Immediately in front of the villa is a large green esplanade used for exercising the horses; to the east is a series of elegant open-air garden rooms, first seen from before the house as an enticing cross-axis — a pier-framed vista disappearing in perspective. The spaces seem to be carved out of woodlands, delineated by high walls of clipped yew, and are a priceless study in classical proportions when seen on plan. The first compartment, or green salon, is about 40 metres wide and three squares in length. The length is equally divided between a flowered parterre garden and a balustraded water rectangle culminating in a Baroque fantasy with giants. The cross-axis continues across the water and, after a short rising corridor, enters a circular ante-room with a pool and fountain. Continuing through a similar corridor, it finally enters what many consider the most beautiful as well as the best preserved open-air garden theatre in Italy. The auditorium is semicircular, the stage recedes with wings and backcloth, and the whole is encompassed within a circle whose centre is the prompter's box. The stage is permanently furnished with terracotta statues of Columbine, Harlequin and Pulcinella; thus even without an audience it is evocative of its past. (*Oxford Companion to Gardens*)

Colour plates pages 118 and 119

continued

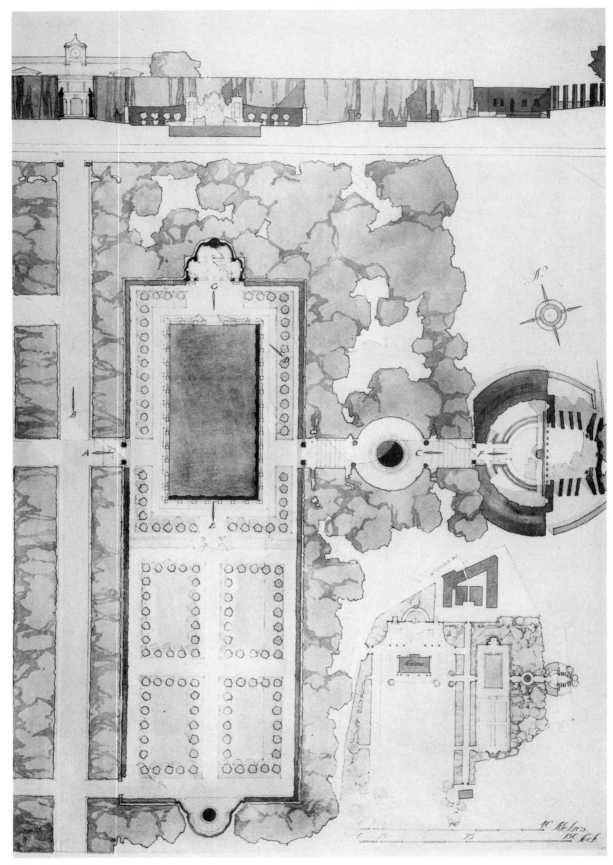

Plan Villa Marlia

Villa Marlia, Lucca

continued

Villa Marlia, Lucca

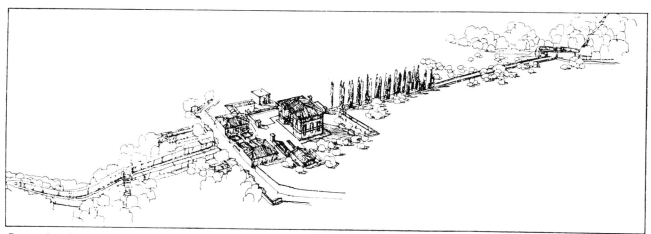

Perspective sketch

Villa Cetinale, near Siena
(1680. Architect Carlo Fontana)

The two estates of Cetinale and Cuzzano are a study in Baroque exploration of linear space. The architect of the former, Carlo Fontana, was a pupil of Bernini; mainly known for his church design, he was also responsible for many small country villas. Cetinale lies eight miles from Siena and its park extends in a thin straight line across agricultural land to finish in a climb to a hermit's retreat. This is not a traditional avenue in which space is indecisive, but one of a series of proportions that generate the energy that is the essence of Baroque art. The culmination of linear perspective is seen at Valzanzibio (pages 151-153).

continued

Villa Cetinale, near Siena

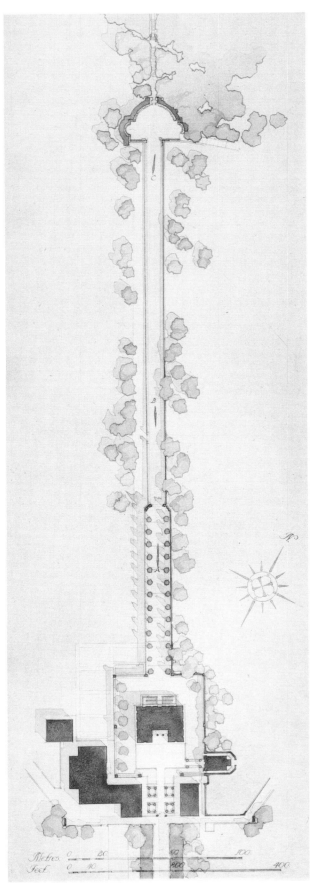

Plan Villa Cetinale

Villa Crivelli, Inverigo
(Late 17th century)

The linear concept now stands free and a monument in its own right. The Scala del Gigante (called after the gigantic statue of Hercules that terminates one end) sweeps for a kilometre across the agricultural landscape, taking on the way the villa, its gardens and a farm house.

The straight line is the stamp of human authority on the countryside, either inhuman as with an avenue, or humanised as it is here.

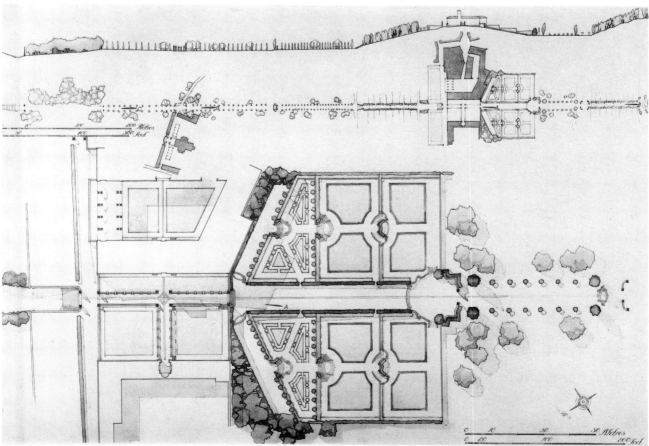

Section and plan

continued

Villa Crivelli, Inverigo

Villa Cuzzano, near Verona
(Late 17th century)

The idea behind Cuzzano is similar to that of its contemporary Poggio Torselli in Tuscany (pages 106-107), for both compositions rely upon a view terrace as their culmination. Whereas, however, the latter is firm and assured Renaissance and the landscape outside is *observed,* that of Cuzzano is loosely Baroque and *partakes* of the countryside.

The design of the parterre, which is original, is probably unique in Italy because of its reflection of the lines of the vineyards on the hillside opposite, and is clearly of French influence. For one who remembers pacing the parterre it does not seem that the design as shown is of the quality and character that its site deserves. This may have been the fault of the pacer, for curves (as opposed to straight lines) are anathema to the pacer and therefore may have been incorrectly interpreted.

continued

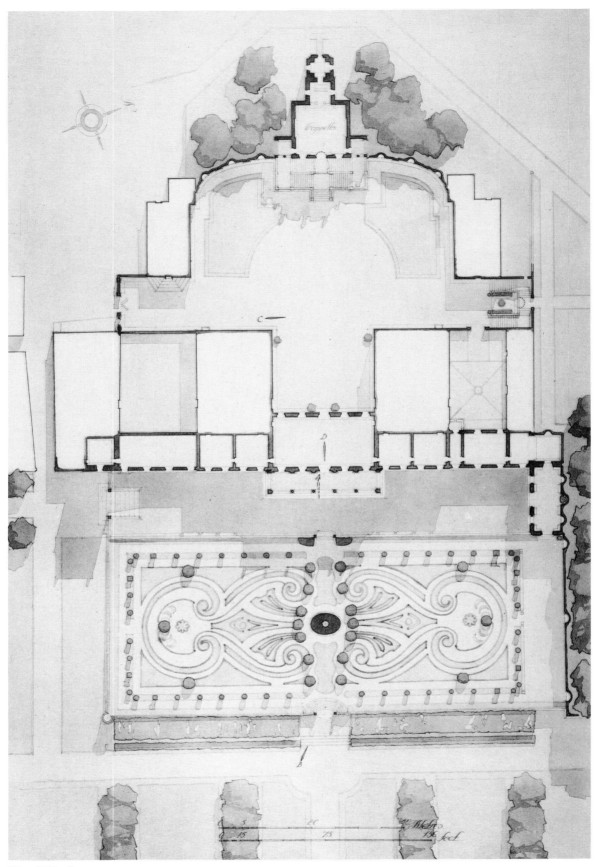

Plan Villa Cuzzano

Villa Cuzzano, Verona

Villa Geggiano, garden theatre

Left and right: Villa Gori, near Siena

Perspective sketch

Villa Dona dalle Rose, Valzanzibio
(Begun by Antonio Barbarigo, Procurator of Venice, c.1690)

All gardens are composed of myth and reality but none more so than that of the Villa Dona dalle Rose. The site is an amphitheatre of hills commanding the flat plains of the Venito.

The *myth* is Virgilian. Great nature that formed the hills gives forth its life-giving waters to descend in sculptured pools to the heroic watergate, entry to the canals that lead to Venice. If you yourself as a grandee entered here (which is probable as you would be coming by boat and thinking the entrance were for you) you would soon be aware that you are only part, and a very small part, of creation.

The *reality* has formed the cross-axis planned solely for man himself: the diminished perspective designed optically for the human eye, the practical layout of shady walks and the useful enclosures, the cypress avenues that link this man-made phenomenon to the hills.

This garden, the first we surveyed, could be paced reasonably easily because of the straight lines. The maze is accurate.

Section

continued

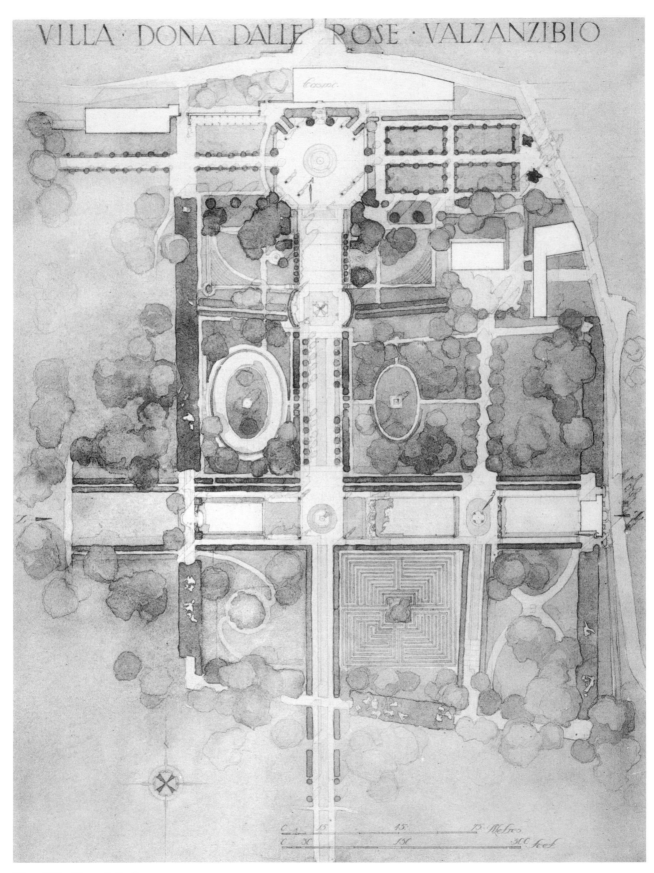

VILLA · DONA DALLE ROSE · VALZANZIBIO

Plan Villa Dona dalle Rose

152

Villa Dona dalle Rose, Valzanzibio

Collegio Rosa, Spello
(15th century; 1808. Attributed to Giuseppe Piermarini)

The layout depicts the beginning and end of the historic Italian garden movements. The early nineteenth century layout, attributed to the architect of La Scala, Milan, suggests the fanciful decorative touch of the theatre, and is composed as a feature in its own right. By reason of the low tone values of the shadows, this is possibly the only drawing where the form of reality is uneasily conveyed.

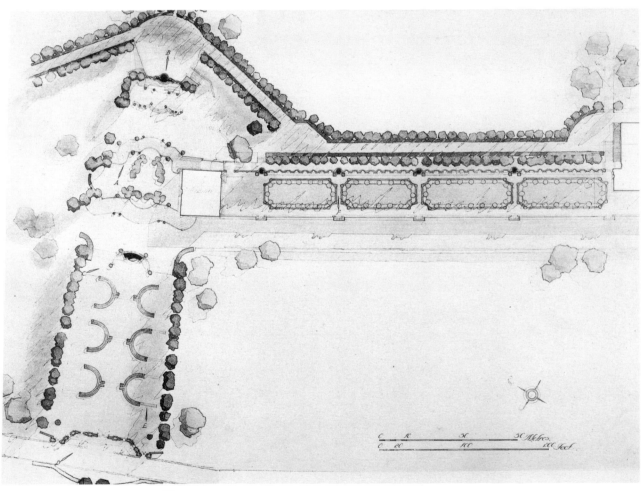

Plan

continued

155

Collegio Rosa, Spello

BIBLIOGRAPHY

Italian Gardens of the Renaissance, J.C. Shepherd and G.A. Jellicoe, London 1925.

Italian Gardens, Georgina Masson, London 1961, Woodbridge 1987.

The Landscape of Man, Geoffrey and Susan Jellicoe, London 1975; paperback 1982.

The Guelph Lectures on Landscape Design, Geoffrey Jellicoe, University of Guelph 1983.

Oxford Companion to Gardens, G.A. Jellicoe, S. Jellicoe, P. Goode, M.L. Lancaster, Oxford 1986.

The Landscape of Civilisation, Geoffrey Jellicoe, Woodbridge, 1989.

BAROQUE
GARDENS OF AUSTRIA

The undertaking of this work was made possible through the Bernard Webb Studentship at the British School at Rome. I wish also to acknowledge with gratitude the assistance of all in Austria and England who helped towards its completion.

In particular, the finish of the drawings is by Alison Shepherd.

G.A. Jellicoe, London, December 1931

NOTE TO 1993 EDITION
This edition is without alteration to the original. It was while trying to emulate J.C. Shepherd's drawing in *Italian Gardens of the Renaissance* in Salzburg that I decided I was no draughtsman and never would be. The study is one of pure history as interpreted at the time. The photography is mine. The colour plates all modern.

CONTENTS

INTRODUCTION

Austria became a first class power at the end of the seventeenth century. Though her society was at this time composed of elements from every part of Europe, her character was sufficiently strong to absorb only the knowledge she required, and from this to form her culture. If Italy and France, Spain and Netherlands, Turkey and North Africa, were echoed at Vienna, the stamp was that of the Habsburg dynasty. In garden design the sphere of Austria is limited to the age in which she flourished, and in contrast with Italy the part which she played is brief and spectacular.

I

The Italian Garden

The origins of all Renaissance garden design are found in Italy in the fourteenth century. For four centuries the progress of thought was continuous, passing from phase to phase, and during her decline Italy bequeathed to wealthier nations an art they were quick to acclimatise. The individuality of the Italian villa seems to express not only the personal independence of the owner, but the condition of a country divided into a number of small states. The garden was considered a place of relaxation, a joyous extension of the villa in nature, a cool and shady series of spaces. Climate largely precluded flowers, and the interest lay in sculpture and foliage. The design being based upon a balance between man and nature, the composition conformed not only with the immediate ground but with the scale and character of the whole landscape. This often gave rise to an irregular plan, the lines of which possibly grew less formal as they receded from the house. Though in later gardens, such as those at Frascati near Rome, the intimacy between man and nature became less apparent, the sense of relation to site was retained. By the seventeenth century the emotions suggested by nature were consciously brought into architecture. Fountains echoed the curves of water; gardens drew their surroundings into their midst; the terraces of the lake gardens rose horizontally from the surface of the water. The secret of this art of Baroque lies in the sense of unity and control beneath a theatrical front, and from the vigorous sculpture of Bernini to his colonnade for St. Peter's the art is supreme. By the end of the century Rome must have presented to Austrian travellers a brilliant spectacle of pomp and magnificence.

The French Garden

The same period saw the rise of Louis XIV, and the centre of culture in Europe moved from Italy to France. Paris was the city round which the affairs of a nation revolved. Her buildings expressed the triumph of the monarch. Vaux le Vicomte, the first of the series of gardens by Le Nôtre, was finished in 1661, and astonished the world with what seemed a new art in garden design. Since the time of Francis I France had been influenced by Italy, but the main inspirations of Le Nôtre were the avenues and forests with their hunting tradition, and a fascination for water that had once attracted the court to the Loire. To the world the success of Vaux lay in the space for fêtes, the vast parterres, canals, fountains, statues, bosquets, the dramatic setting for a court. Such gardens were for the relaxation not of an individual but of a multitude. In design the significance of Vaux is the sense of pattern, and the development into form along an undulating landscape. Versailles itself was a web spun of palace, dependencies, and gardens. With an outlook on nature more imperious than the Italian, Le Nôtre spread beyond the confines of the park with avenues and vistas, and, as with the view over the Orangery at Versailles towards the Satory woods, drew into the heart of the garden any part of the landscape he desired. For over a century the French conception of a garden dominated Europe, and French landscape artists were invited everywhere.

While Italy and France had thus advanced, the German Empire was far behind. Austria, virtual head of the States, adjoined north-east Italy, and lay on a main trade route between Europe, Constantinople and the East. Her position was at once her weakness and her strength, for Vienna was the bulwark against the Turk; though fear of invasion checked her expansion, it tended to raise her above the other states as their natural protector.

The Traditional German Garden

Early in the sixteenth century the Habsburg lands under Maximilian I were spread over Austria, Hungary, Bohemia, and the Tyrol. Helped by the Reformation and the humanist revival, the Renaissance began to penetrate across the Alps. Possibly there were more gardens in Germany during the sixteenth century than in any country in Europe except Italy. The science of horticulture developed rapidly; travellers told of the Italian garden; and the first German book on garden design, the work of Johann Peschel, appeared in 1597. Owing to the unsettled conditions, gardens were rarely made outside the walls of towns and castles. They were decked with some of the superficial delights of the Italian garden, but retained the old sense of enclosure. The arrangement of sports grounds, flower beds, arbors, was a simple reflection of the rooms of the house; and if nature in the form of landscape played any part it was as a distant picture. Every castle had its garden, and at times this reached gigantic proportions. The famous gardens of Heidelberg, by Salomon de Caus, exceeded in expanse of parterre and size of earthworks anything even in Italy. In Austria itself there are numerous finely situated castles with here and there the remains of a garden, or, as at Rosenberg, a tilting-yard. The

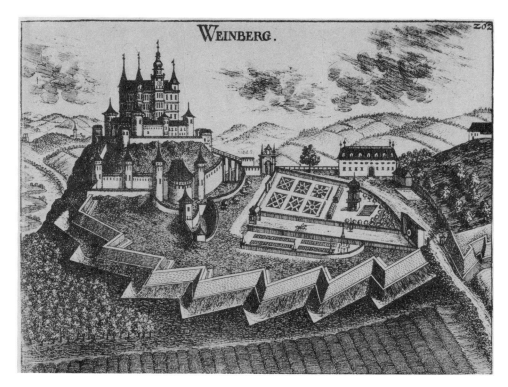

Prints of early Austrian gardens — Weinberg, Erlach and Neugebaude

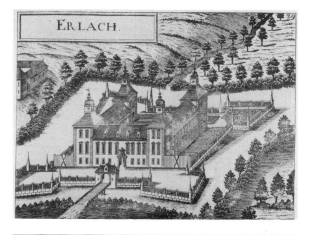

Imperial palace of Neugebaude outside Vienna, built between 1564 and 1575 and now a crematorium, is definitely of the Renaissance. This was a building with gardens laid out primarily for pleasure and fortified through necessity (above).

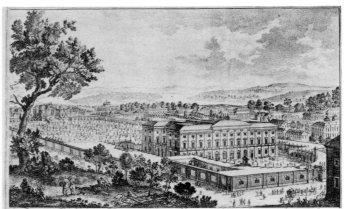

Contemporary prints of eighteenth century Austrian gardens — Trauston, Liechtenstein, St. Joseph, Neuwaldech

Paintings by Bellotto of the grounds of Liechtenstein Palace

Schloss Hellbrunn

Salzburg is now an Austrian province, but before the nineteenth century it was an independent ecclesiastical principality. The Prince Archbishops were in close touch with Italy, and the opening of the seventeenth century found them ambitious enough to try to 'bring Italy across the Alps', to make Salzburg a rival of Rome itself. Though they failed to realize their dream, they created through the Italian architect Santino Solari an early Baroque city. Much of the personal charm of the Tuscan garden is found at Hellbrunn, laid out in 1613-15, a few miles from Salzburg. As far removed from the great gardens of the following century as is the intimacy of Salzburg from the imperiousness of Vienna, it is one of the few places where snow-clad peaks and mountain trees intermingle with a Renaissance garden. The plan itself is immature, the parts are unrelated, the garden detail is bad, and the quaint conceits with which it abounds, rather trivial. In this triviality, as well as in the affinity to nature, lies the charm.

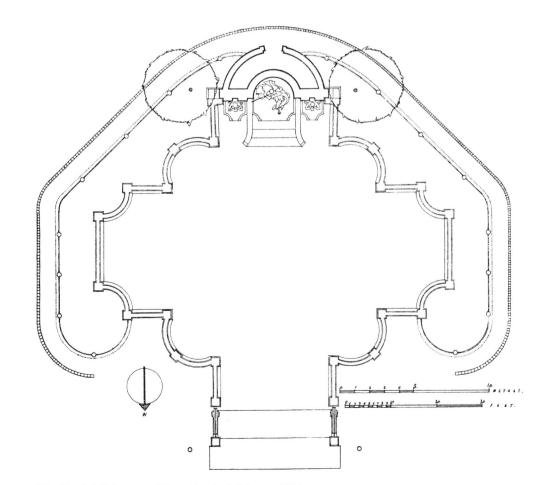

The Kapitel-Schwemme Horse Pond, Salzburg, 1732

Count Wallenstein's Garden

The Thirty Years' War broke out in 1618 and the whole of Germany was torn by what began as a religious, and ended as a political conflict. The progress of culture was stopped and distress was felt for years. During the struggle the redoubtable warrior Count Wallenstein retired and, building himself a palace in the heart of Prague, filled an awkward site with a garden, half medieval and half Italian (pages 188-9). The ingenious plan is thrown out of scale by the loggia, which may possibly have been intended to face a longer vista; and the effect of the whole is incongruous though attractive. Though Prague as the capital of Bohemia was in close touch with Vienna, this solitary achievement has little bearing on the course of garden design in Austria.

Following the Peace of Westphalia, Austria became involved in wars with the Turks on one side, and Louis XIV on the other. Despite the interest in the arts taken by successive Habsburgs, the Renaissance made little headway. Towards the end of the century the plight of Austria became desperate, and in 1683 Vienna was invested by the Turkish army. The loss of Vienna threatened all Europe, but was averted by the Poles under John Sobieski. The siege was raised, the Turks were routed, and the whole country seemed to awake from a stupor. Under Prince Eugene of Savoy, a brilliant general who had once offered his services to Louis XIV, the country generally came into the forefront of European politics. At the end of the century the second defeat of the Turks at Zenta finally broke the Ottoman power, and the new age was clear.

II

Historical

Politically the age extended under Leopold I (1657-1705), Joseph I (1705-11), Charles VI (1711-40), and Maria Theresa (1740-80). Though the War of the Spanish Succession (1701-14) lost Spain to the Habsburgs, it added to their possessions. The supremacy of Louis XIV was over, and Austria was apparently the first power in Europe. In reality she was far from stable.[1] Maria Theresa ascended the throne of a vast empire that was on the verge of collapse. The Empress, whose right of succession had been secured by the Pragmatic Sanction, proved herself perhaps the greatest ruler of her line.

1. 'At the conclusion of the Quadruple Alliance, Charles seems to have attained the summit of his power and splendour; and if we estimate his power from his possessions he would appear the greatest monarch in Christendom. He was by election Emperor of Germany, by hereditary right sovereign of Hungary, Transylvania, Bohemia, Austria, Styria, Carinthia, and Carniola, the Tyrol, and the Brisgau, and he had recently obtained Naples and Sicily, the Milanese and the Netherlands. The population of these extensive dominions did not amount to less than 24,000,000 of souls. But if we consider the effective strength of these territories and their disjointed state, we shall find that Charles was rather weakened than strengthened by his new acquisitions.' Coxe, *History of the House of Austria.*

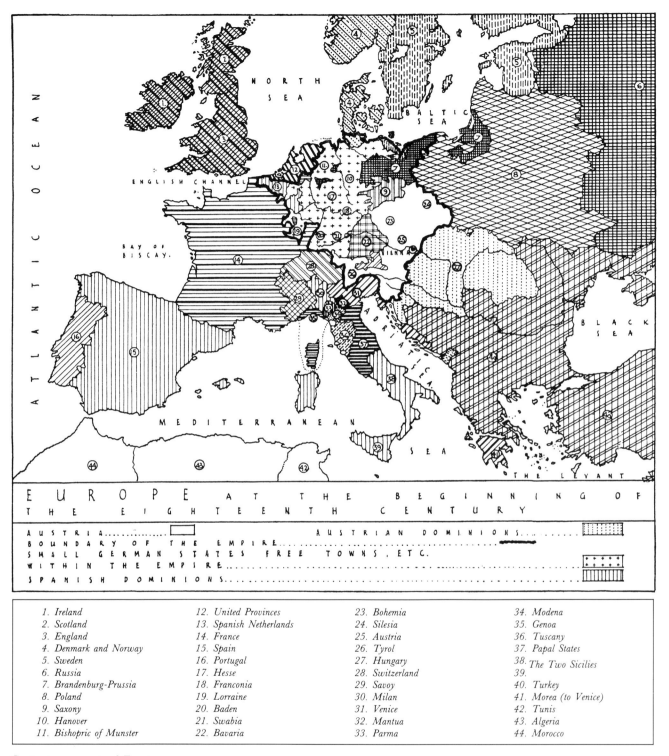

Contemporary map of Europe at the beginning of the eighteenth century

EUROPE AT THE BEGINNING OF THE EIGHTEENTH CENTURY

AUSTRIA ....
AUSTRIAN DOMINIONS ....
BOUNDARY OF THE EMPIRE ....
SMALL GERMAN STATES FREE TOWNS, ETC.
WITHIN THE EMPIRE ....
SPANISH DOMINIONS ....

1. Ireland	12. United Provinces	23. Bohemia	34. Modena
2. Scotland	13. Spanish Netherlands	24. Silesia	35. Genoa
3. England	14. France	25. Austria	36. Tuscany
4. Denmark and Norway	15. Spain	26. Tyrol	37. Papal States
5. Sweden	16. Portugal	27. Hungary	38. The Two Sicilies
6. Russia	17. Hesse	28. Switzerland	39.
7. Brandenburg-Prussia	18. Franconia	29. Savoy	40. Turkey
8. Poland	19. Lorraine	30. Milan	41. Morea (to Venice)
9. Saxony	20. Baden	31. Venice	42. Tunis
10. Hanover	21. Swabia	32. Mantua	43. Algeria
11. Bishopric of Munster	22. Bavaria	33. Parma	44. Morocco

Leopold I

The Court of Leopold I was a scene of activity. For the moment Vienna became the centre of interest in Europe, and attracted statesmen and artists of all nationalities. The same spirit sent Austrian travellers into most of the courts of Europe, exploring contemporary knowledge and fashions. Enmity with Louis XIV did not obscure the fact that the power of 'Le Roi Soleil' was reflected in the magnificence of Paris and Versailles. Vienna, the city of music, was to become a city of all the arts. Building took place on a scale gigantic for so small a community; even the religious orders blossomed as the Church triumphant rather than militant. The age was one of theatrical art, but behind the scenery and costumes of the actors lay the associations of the past. Change of politics could not in a moment throw off centuries of feudalism and fortress walls.

Notable Families

With the Emperor lay the enthusiasm of individuals. The most influential was Prince Eugene, whose friendship and close association with Cardinal Alessandro Albani may have inspired much of his love of building. His campaigns took him over North Italy, while intimacy with the Duke of Marlborough during the Wars of the Spanish Succession brought him for a brief period to the English court. Here he may have met Vanbrugh, the theatrical designer and architect of Blenheim Palace. He was a lavish patron of the arts, passionately fond of garden design, and stands to Austrian garden art as to her politics. Among the statesmen, the astute Adam von Liechtenstein was not only a patron of the arts but a connoisseur. He was associated with Spain and Rome, and after building a winter and summer palace, furnished the latter with one of the finest private collections of pictures in existence. Less spectacular but of wider influence upon the course of garden art was the Schonborn family. Branches linked Vienna with all parts of Germany. The head of the family was the garden enthusiast Lothar Franz von Schonborn, Bishop of Bamberg in 1693, and Archbishop-Elector of Mainz in 1695.

Italian Architects

The Italians who crossed the Alps by invitation brought with them a technical scenic ability, the architects being as well equipped as the theatrical designers themselves. Of the former, Domenico Martinelli was probably the greatest. He was a native of Lucca, made his name in Rome, and attracted the attention of von Liechtenstein, for whom he built both palaces. He appears to have carried out little garden design, but his influence on detail was profound.[2] Another architect was Donato Felice d'Allio, who built the Salesian Nunnery and altered the monastery of Klosterneuburg. Both are as well designed as anything in Austria. Of the scenic designers the Bibiena family working in Bavaria were the most famous. In Vienna L.O. Burnacini designed theatrical scenery, the monument in the Graben, and the Imperial palace of Favorita (now the Theresian Academy). Of architectural draughtsmen the best was Andrea Pozzo. In the train of the Italians came the craftsmen, men who set a standard of technique as high as at any time.

2. He was arbitrary, and after further building retired to Lucca, where possibly he built the Villa Sardi, the garden features of which are reminiscent of the Belvedere.

Other Foreign Architects

The relationship of Austria to the fellow states of Germany was one of superiority. The states sparred among themselves, and each preserved the independence that had marked them for centuries. There were over three hundred free states or cities at this period and their art is varied and interesting. The larger and more wealthy called in Italians if they leaned towards Austria, or Frenchmen if towards France. The most ambitious of all was Maximilian of Bavaria, a refugee at the court of Louis XIV from 1704 to 1714. The two palaces of Nymphenburg and Schleissheim, near Munich, were undertakings each with a huge park. Their French influence is clear for both were inspired by François Girard, a pupil of Le Nôtre. Girard was one of the few Frenchmen to be called to Vienna, and in the Belvedere gardens for Prince Eugene produced in collaboration the finest garden design in Austria. Among native German architects of the first class who may have a bearing on Austrian design was J.B. Neumann and K. A. Dientzenhofer. Both were associated with the Schonborn family. Neumann, apart from church work, built the great Schloss at Wurzburg. Though Dientzenhofer claimed to have built the palace of Pommersfelden for the Schonborn family,[3] his most charming work is the little Concordia palace and garden on the river at Bamberg.

Austrian Architects

For a time the influx of foreigners into Vienna was such as to overwhelm native talent, and buildings must have risen on all sides to the sound of foreign tongues. From this medley there appeared two Austrians who came almost to monopolise work, Fischer von Erlach and Lukas von Hildebrandt.

Fischer von Erlach

Johann Bernard Fischer von Erlach was born at Graz in 1657. From 1680-5 he studied in Rome and North Italy, making drawings for a series of engravings published in 1721. These were for the most part imaginative reconstructions, and the book *Entwurff einer historischen Architektur* was a unique preparation for his later work. Besides Italian examples, there are many from the near East. In Rome itself Bernini had just died (1680), and the most illustrious architect was Carlo Fontana. The impression of contemporary Rome on Fischer's young mind gave his work a strength peculiar to himself. The gardens at Frascati presented an impressive sight, while in North Italy he prepared an engraving of Isola Bella on Lake Maggiore. On returning to Vienna his first commission was to carry out the design of Burnacini for the Graben monument. This extravaganza is a key to Baroque, for beneath apparent chaos lies a sense of order. For a time he worked in the Belvedere under the painter Louis Dorigny. His first large work was the University Church in Salzburg; the earliest design for the palace of Schönbrunn,

3. From family records and the character of the work this was probably built by Hildebrandt.

abandoned through expense, was made in 1696. From this date he carried out many public buildings and churches, a few palaces in or around Vienna, and one or two farther afield, especially at Prague. He was an idealist and his intractable temper often caused trouble with his clients, a notable person with whom he once fell out being Prince Eugene. Perhaps it was traceable to this peculiarity that he was less of a domestic architect than Hildebrandt. He died in 1723, the practice being continued by a son. To Fischer is largely due the stability that Austrian design maintained in spite of so many influences. He was a planner of the highest class. He thought and worked in three dimensions, always remembering the dramatic, and was the only architect Austria produced who may claim a worldwide reputation.

Garden House at Kleissheim, near Salzburg, by Fischer von Erlach

Lukas von Hildebrandt

Johann Lukas von Hildebrandt was born in 1666 at Genoa. More of a courtier and less of an architect than Fischer, he applied himself lightly to classical and contemporary Italian study. His work for the palaces of the nobility was abundant, and in this respect he appears to have outshone Fischer. His practice extended over Austria, Bohemia, and south east Germany, where he worked for the Schonborn family. He brought to his designs a brisk imagination, a superficial knowledge of the classics, bad detail, and a sense of planning and grouping. He died in 1745, and with him closed the main Baroque era.

Austrian Materials

By this array of designers both native and foreign the stage was then set with scenery. Owing to the proximity of the Alps many of the western towns, including Salzburg, are pleasant mainly in July and August. Vienna on the other hand, though noted for its breezes, is too hot during these months. Heat and wind promoted hedge planting, for which soil and climate offered the widest scope. The planting of hornbeam, chestnut, maple, beech, lime, and sycamore, as well as the smaller scale yew and box, have produced the grandest clipped hedges and avenues. Juniper and acacia were used for variety. The most prolific forest trees were larches, firs, and Siberian pines, and deciduous trees for such plantations as those at Schönbrunn, were oak, ash, beech and elm. The cypress was never planted. Of fruit trees, besides the more common variety such as apple, there were fig, olive, almond, lemon, and pomegranate. Lemon trees were used decoratively in pots. Turf was not an integral part of every garden, as in England, and was not used for its design value even so much as in France. This was possibly due to affinity to Italy, where grass could only be grown with difficulty, and took little part in garden design. The best planting today is in the Mirabell gardens in Salzburg, but even here the flowers do not seem so happy as in the gardens of southern Germany. The parterre at Schönbrunn is planted in gaily coloured patterns; the flower sense is lost. In the great entertaining gardens the scene was laid among dark hedges, grey stone, and gravel; they were settings not for flowers but for the highly costumed actors themselves. This is a characteristic of the age.

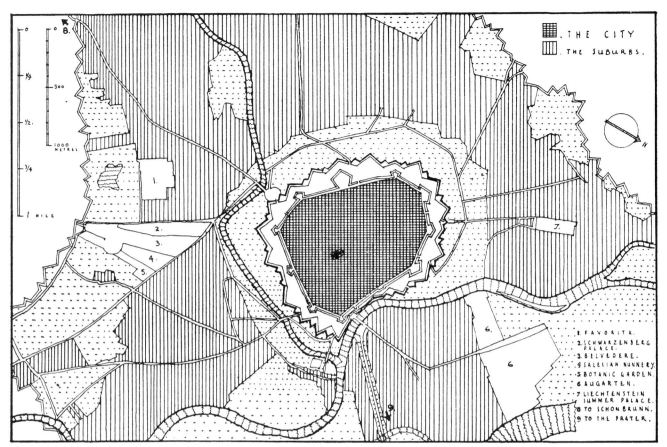

1. FAVORITA.
2. SCHWARZENBERG PALACE.
3. BELVEDERE.
4. SALESIAN NUNNERY.
5. BOTANIC GARDEN.
6. AUGARTEN.
7. LIECHTENSTEIN SUMMER PALACE.
8. TO SCHONBRUNN.
9. TO THE PRATER.

Vienna about the middle of the eighteenth century, from a contemporary map

III

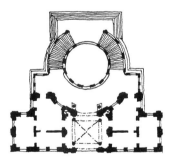

Liechtenstein Belvedere, Vienna

The Stage

The eighteenth century map of Vienna (above) shows a strongly walled city having a girdle of open land, and beyond this the suburbs. This girdle is now the Ring. Gardens that had existed before 1683, such as Schönbrunn, were destroyed by the Turks. Exceptions were Neugebaude (page 163), occupied by the Sultan during the siege; the Prater, mainly an avenue of chestnuts, two and a half miles long, first planted in 1537 and now as always a pleasure centre; and the Augarten (1650), an imperial lay-out of clipped avenues showing a knowledge of composition.

The city lies on an arm of the Danube, the river itself making no contribution to the general plan. On three sides, south, west and north, the ground slopes gently upwards. From these slopes in 1683 the place presented every aspect of a medieval town, of crowded dwellings behind immense fortifications. In the centre the single spire of St. Stephen's rose isolated above the smaller towers of parish churches. To the west and the north-west were the sandstone hills of the Wiener Wald, covered with vineyards, meadows and woods, forming a perpetual background to views from the south. Impulse of building caused rapid expansion beyond the walls, and it was not long before a summer palace outside the city became as fashionable as one within. Not only were the slopes cooler, but they gave a view over the city with the open land as foreground and in turn were themselves places of display.

172

The Imperial villa of Favorita, now the Theresian Academy, was laid out by L.O. Burnacini soon after 1683, and came to be the favourite residence of Joseph I; only a few avenues of chestnuts exist today of what can never have been an interesting garden, but the modelling of the ground to the south suggests an appreciation of the outlook. Undoubtedly the view was better from the south of the city than from the north. The first of the great summer palaces on the north was that begun in 1697 by Domenico Martinelli for Prince von Liechtenstein (pages 164 and 165). This remains the finest of any in Vienna. The garden with its Belvedere (page 172), both recently destroyed, was laid out by Fischer von Erlach. South of the city lies an awkward shaped area governed by roads, upon which stands a series of buildings and gardens still almost intact. The Schwarzenberg palace was begun in 1697 and completed about 1715 by Fischer von Erlach; the Belvedere palaces were built (1714-25) by Hildebrandt; and the Salesian Nunnery, the garden of which is not well preserved (right), by Donato Felice D'Allio in 1717-30. Beyond, the Botanic Garden was founded in 1754. The erection of palaces and gardens outside the Ring was extensive. Some of the buildings, like the Trauston palace, by Fischer von Erlach, now the Palace of the Hungarian Lifeguards (page 164), have lost only their gardens. The majority have been swallowed up in modern Vienna, and only churches, the lines of roads, a few buildings here and there, and odd details such as piers and gates, indicate the contemporary city. The palace of the Hofburg was rebuilt by Fischer von Erlach, and the design of Hildebrandt for a garden on the ramparts (page 174) was never carried out. Schönbrunn lies about 2½ miles west from the city gates of the Hofburg.

The Schwarzenberg and Belvedere palaces between them embrace the whole art of Austrian Baroque garden design. Although Girard is described as a water engineer, and was only a collaborator with

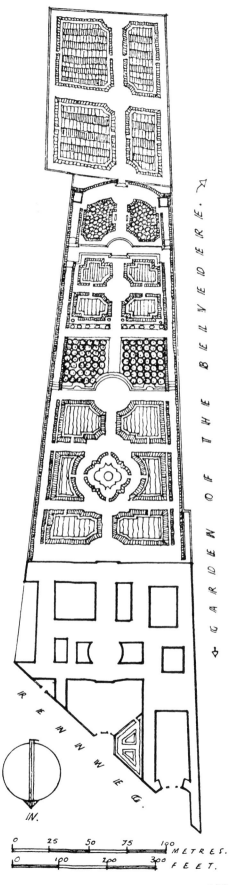

The Salesian Nunnery, Vienna, reconstructed from a plan by Salomon Kleiner. The main lines are still in existence

173

Hildebrandt over the Belvedere garden, other work assigned to both individually indicates that his was the moving spirit. Both Nymphenburg and Schleissheim with their canals and grouping of trees suggest the work of a pupil of Le Nôtre, and the latter with its two palaces is the germ of the Belvedere composition.

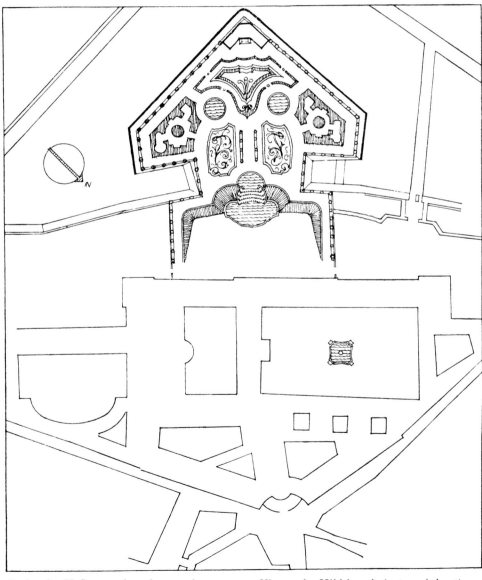

Design for Hofburg and gardens on the ramparts, Vienna, by Hildebrandt (not carried out)

Belvedere and Schwarzenberg

The Belvedere (pages 195-202) consists of a lower and an upper palace, the latter the more sumptuous. The Menagerie and lay-out beyond the upper are well planned for their site, but the most vital portion is that lying between the two palaces. In contrast to that of its neighbour, the site is here rectangular and there is no need for the ingenuity that marks the Schwarzenberg. The recognition of the garden as a link between the two buildings is the key to the plan; the walks along each boundary are not only the main ways from one palace to the other, but the architectural ties between the two. Down the middle lies the contrast, cascade, pools, parterre, sculpture, the concentration at special points beautifully arranged. The placing of the paths to the sides adds to the sense of size (for a centre way divides a single space into two), and gives in addition cross views of the main features. In plan the Schwarzenberg (pages 192-194) with its well proportioned shapes and curves is equally good. The superiority of the Belvedere over all other Austrian gardens lies in its sense of modelling and relation to the swell of the land. The twin walks that link the palaces follow the rising ground. Within this frame, and introduced by degrees of slopes, the ground is carved away to a level parterre. The upper palace is grouped to suggest continuity and a fitting culmination. Though the detail of the building itself is poor, and the form hesitating, the scene is one of the most dramatic in existence. The terrace before the Upper Belvedere is the viewpoint for the Vienna basin. The foreground descends in horizontal planes between frames that fall with the slopes of the rim, the pools reflect the sky and draw together 'the dome of the heavens and earth,' the lower palace is simple, and beyond is a view little changed from that depicted by Bellotto (page 194).

Relation of House and Garden

Although the relation between the interior of the house and the garden was close, the principal suite of rooms was as a rule on the first floor. Access to the garden, as at the Schwarzenberg and Schönbrunn, was often by means of a central garden stair. The views from the windows were carefully considered to give both intimacy and distance. This is a characteristic that appears at Hellbrunn, where the views of the pools contrast with those of the Alps, and continues until the time of Schönbrunn, where the Kammergarten contrasts with the Gloriette. The French garden being more impersonal, rarely lays such variety of scale before the palace.

Beyond the environs of Vienna a number of palaces and gardens were built. Among these Eckartsau (by Hildebrandt 1720), Hetzendorf (by Pacassi, 1744, the Italian who continued with the palace of Schönbrunn), and Laxenburg (1754), all imperial residences, were perhaps the most important.

Farther afield many smaller buildings, such as Guillenstein, have charming garden details. In partial preservation are the palaces of Schonborn (pages 203-204) by Hildebrandt, and Schlosshof (pages 210-212). Both schemes indicate a limitation of the Austrian garden. These places were oases of court

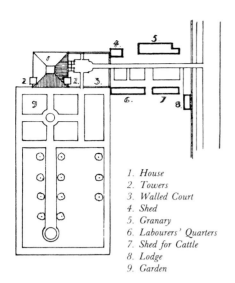

1. House
2. Towers
3. Walled Court
4. Shed
5. Granary
6. Labourers' Quarters
7. Shed for Cattle
8. Lodge
9. Garden

Plan of Schloss Weisbach, Hallein, from a model

Plan of Schloss Frohnburg, near Salzburg, attributed to Santino Solari

1. House
2. Entrance Lodge
3. Flower Garden
4. Orchard
5. Outbuildings
6. Pool
7. Garden House
8. Water Tower
9. Barn
10. Kitchen Garden

life. They are approached through fairly pleasant country, yet within their own gates they are independent of their surroundings. The country is a painted backcloth. There is none of the tender sympathy for nature felt by the Italians, nor the forceful expansion into it by Le Nôtre. The gardens are confined precisely to their rectangle, and are as much divorced from the countryside, as for practical reasons were the medieval castles and gardens.

Influence of Tradition

The extent to which tradition underlay design is more clearly seen in the smaller houses and gardens that were associated with the land. Schloss Weisbach at Hallein (above left) is a typical establishment. Near Salzburg, Frohnburg (above right) is reputed to have been built by Solari, but the lay-out is a rearrangement of house and farm buildings. Meidling-im-Thal, near Gottweig, is later in date than Frohnburg and is more definitely a farm; beneath some light touches of Baroque lies a garden that might have been laid out, had conditions allowed, before the Thirty Years' War.[4]

4. In the Kaiser-Zimmer of the monastery close by are several paintings of small houses and farms and gardens, all of this character.

Mirabell Gardens

The most pronounced example of a Baroque design rising on medieval form are the Mirabell gardens at Salzburg (pages 205-209), of which the palace was rebuilt by Hildebrandt and the garden possibly designed by Fischer von Erlach. The lay-out was controlled by the existing ramparts, but the main view towards the castle of Hohensalzburg follows the idea of the Belvedere and links the garden to the town. These gardens are more in keeping with the scale and traditions of Salzburg than are those of Klessheim (below) about six miles away, built by Fischer von Erlach about 1700-9. Here is a monumental layout on a flat site in the typical grand manner, the most human parts of which are the outbuildings and little garden houses.

Monasteries

The true landscape architecture of the Austrian Baroque lies in the monasteries. Monastery vied with monastery in magnificence. The situations are usually lofty and spectacular, the florid towers rising above their bastions like flowers from a crag. Melk (rebuilt by Jakob Prandauer 1703-49), crowns a rock above the Danube, and is the equal of any piece of landscape

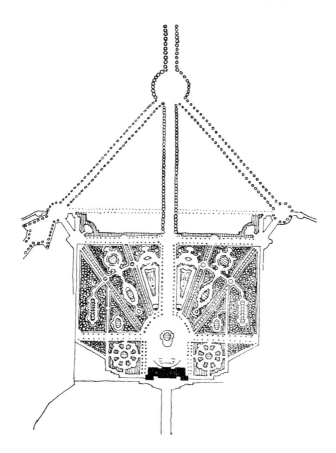

Reconstructed plan of Schloss Kleissheim, near Salzburg

architecture in the world. It is significant that the terrace above the river was probably designed by the theatrical artist Antonio Beduzzi. In this splendour of building in alliance with landscape, garden design played little part. Gottweig, a rival to Melk in situation, was begun with unimportant terrace gardens by Hildebrandt (rebuilding after 1719). Melk itself has a charming but simple little garden and garden house at its rear. Kremsmunster (rebuilding carried on from 1630-1759, partially by Jakob Prandauer) has an arcaded fish tank of 1690 (a sequence of five pools) and a garden view pavilion perched high above the valley.

Possibly the best monastic garden of this period is contained within the court of St. Florian (pages 213-214), also mainly built by Prandauer. Often, as at St. Florian, there were courts and small gardens grouped round the exterior.

Schönbrunn

The greatest effort of Austrian Baroque garden art is the imperial palace of Schönbrunn (pages 215-223). All through the chequered history of its design the character persists of the hunting box and forest before destruction by the Turks. The first design of Fischer von Erlach, in 1696, abandoned through expense, placed the building on the hill. The second design bears some relation to the present scheme. Work was discontinued until 1744, when Pacassi completed the palace, and Steckhoven, a Dutch landscape gardener, introduced the canals of the Netherlands. The final design as it stands today, an amalgamation of several ideas, was completed by the Gloriette of J.F. von Hohenburg. The mighty central space recalls the earlier Belvedere. There is little or no finesse in the design, for the effects depend first upon shock, and afterwards upon the charm of intimate walks.

Summary

In a broad survey of European garden art, Austria plays a well-defined part. With the exception of the Belvedere there is no garden that can rank technically with the finest in Italy or France. Possibly the confined city garden (and the consequent treatment of a long rectangular space) was brought a stage further than by Le Nôtre, for as settings the gardens are unequalled. At times the detail is brilliant. The Belvedere excels in wrought ironwork, the Schwarzenberg and Liechtenstein palaces in vases. Sculpture ranges from the worst to the best, the most vigorous being in the Schwarzenberg and Mirabell gardens. Austria represents the culmination of classical garden design in Europe; the curtain drops to lift on the English School of Landscape Gardening. When this in turn embraced Europe, Austria almost withstood the fashion of changing gardens. Laxenberg, near Vienna, was an exception, and Leopoldskron, near Salzburg, was placed in an English Park. Romanticism can be seen at Schönbrunn in the obelisk and sham ruins. The ruins portend the fall of the stage designer and the rise of the painter; the actor becomes spectator.

Chronological Table

Date and Reign	Italy	France	Austria and Germany
1400-1500 Maximilian I (1493-1519)	Carreggi (Florence) Medici (Fiesole) Poggio-a-Cajano (Florence)		
1500-1600 Charles V (1519-1522) Ferdinand I (1522-1564) Maximilian II (1564-1576) Rudolph II (1576-1612)	Madama (Rome) Vatican Gardens (Rome) Vicobello (Siena) Reale, Castello (Florence) Palazzo del Té (Mantua) Boboli Gardens (Florence) Scassi (Genoa) Caprarola (Viterbo) Este (Tivoli) Palladian Villas (Venetia) Lante (Viterbo) Bernardini (Lucca) Aldobrandini (Frascati) Palazzo Doria (Genoa)	Amboise) Blois) Chambourd) Touraine Chenonceaux) etc.) Anet	Ambras (Tyrol) Neugebaude (Vienna)
1600-1700 Matthias (1612-1619) Ferdinand II (1619-1637) Ferdinand III (1637-1657) Peace of Westp- phalia Leopold I (1657-1705) 1683 Siege of Vienna Peace of Karlo- witz	Gamberaia (Florence) Doria Pamfili (Rome) Falconieri (Frascati) Isola Bella (Lake Maggiore) Garzoni, Collodi (Lucca) Gori (Siena) Valzanzibio (Venetia)	Luxembourg (Paris) St. Germain-en-Laye Chateau de Maisons Tuileries gardens (Paris) Vaux-le-Vicomte Chantilly St. Cloud Fontainebleau Sceaux Meudon Versailles Clagny Grand Trianon (Versailles) Marly-Le-Roi	Residence (Munich) Hellbrunn (Salzburg) Heidelberg Count Wallenstein's garden (Prague) Augarten (Vienna) Herrenhausen (Hanover) Favorita (Vienna) Liechtenstein (Vienna)
1700-1750 Joseph I (1705-1711) Charles VI (1711-1740) Treaties of Utrecht and Rastatt Maria Theresa (1740-1780) Peace of Aix-la- Chapelle	Arcadian Academy (Rome) Castellazzo (Milan) Palazzo Pisani, Stra (Venetia) Carlotta (Lake Como) Albani (Rome)	Liancourt	Wilhelmshohe (Cassel) Schwarzenberg (Vienna) Schonborn (near Vienna) Karlsruhe Zwinger (Dresden) Pommersfelden (Bamberg) Belvedere (Vienna) Residence (Wurzburg) Bruhl (Cologne) Schlosshof (near Vienna) Mirabell gardens (Salzburg) Schwetzingen Sans-Souci (Potsdam) Schönbrunn (Vienna)
1750-1800 Peace of Huber- tusburg Joseph II (1780-1790)	Caserta (Naples) Balbienello (Lake Como)	Petit Trianon (Versailles)	Schönbrunn (Menagerie) Veitschocheim (Wurzburg) New Palace (Potsdam)

SCHLOSS HELLBRUNN, SALZBURG

(Garden with menagerie mentioned 1421, enlargements 1479. Present palace and garden built 1613-15 for Marcus Sitticus von Hohenems, Prince-Archbishop of Salzburg 1612-19. Architect Santino Solari. Hydraulic marionette theatre erected 1673)

The palace of Hellbrunn, three miles east of Salzburg, was begun by Marcus Sitticus the Crafty within a year of the overthrow of his uncle Wolf Dietrich. Here the new archbishop amused himself and his guests with quainter conceits than he had seen in Italy. You sat in the water theatre to the north, and jets shot up from nowhere; or you entered the grotto under the house, and were again soaked. The brook gave pressure for hydraulic toys; now a St. George slew his dragon, now some other feat was performed. The marionette theatre was added later; but you enjoyed the stone grotto (one of the earliest garden theatres), and afterwards the climb to the Monat-Schlosschen, said to have been built in a month.

All this was very entertaining, and Marcus Sitticus, with his uncle safe in Hohensalzburg, an amusing host. That the interest may have flagged did not worry the Archbishop, for his guests were there to charm. But undoubtedly the peculiarities of the garden seem to have overcome Solari, who had built the cathedral and was one of the ablest of the Italians outside Italy. The approach, forecourt, and house itself, are dignified; the interior is delightful, and the two water gardens are beautifully disposed before the windows of the main floor. They appear immediately upon the house, and possibly this answers the criticism that house and garden at these points are overcrowded. The state visitor from other countries, whom the more intimate attractions of the gardens might not so much amuse as prejudice, would approach by the avenue from Salzburg, enter the drive at a sharp right angle, descend before the steps, and ascend to the principal suite. From these windows he would have the choice of magnificent views of distant snow clad Alps, or those of the closer pools. If he were from Italy he would probably smile at the small sense of size and the immaturity of the garden details, but would admit their affinity to firs and larches, trees he had probably never seen planted in a garden. In any case he himself would not feel akin.

Colour plate page 186

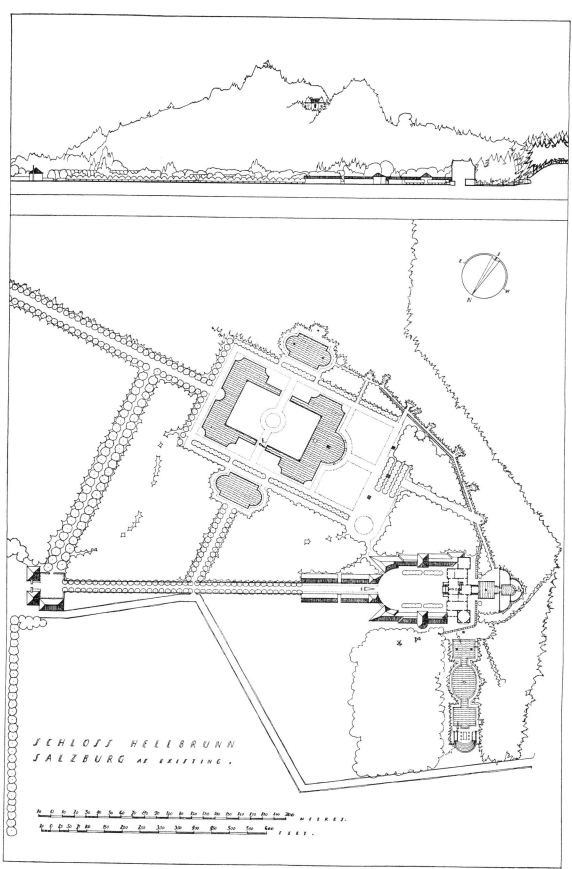

SCHLOSS HELLBRUNN
SALZBURG AS EXISTING.

Plan and section as existing

continued

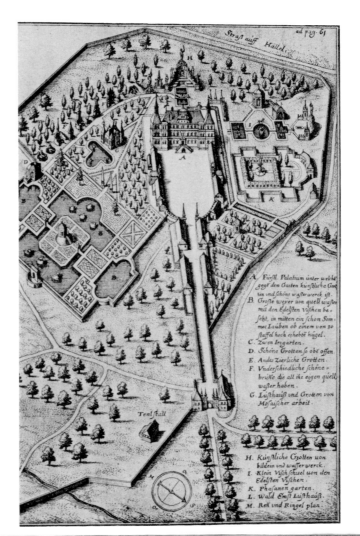

Bird's eye view of Schloss
Hellbrunn from an old
engraving

Schloss Hellbrunn from an engraving by R.A. Danreiter, 1760

Schloss Hellbrunn, Salzburg

continued

Five views of Schloss Hellbrunn, Salzburg

Schloss Hellbrunn,
Salzburg

The Belvedere, Vienna

The Belvedere, Vienna

187

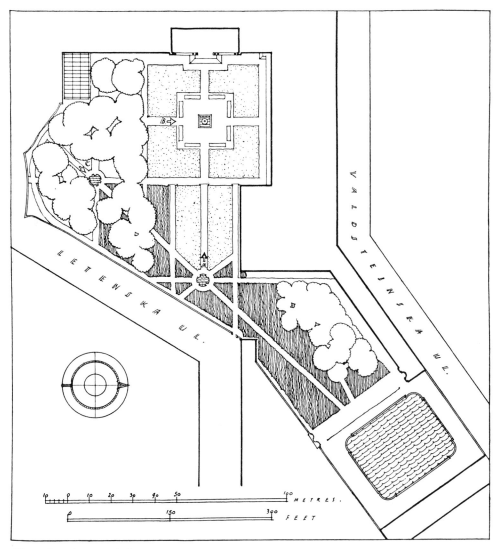

Plan of garden as existing

COUNT WALLENSTEIN'S GARDEN, PRAGUE

(Built 1623-30 by Giovanni Marini of Milan for Count Albrecht von Wallenstein, from plans by Andrea Spezza. Stucco work possibly by Bartolommeo Bianco)

Count Wallenstein, a man of vast wealth and ambitions, and a striking character in history, was a powerful supporter of the Habsburgs in the Thirty Years' War. Retiring for a while during the conflict, he built himself a palace in Prague, and lived in great magnificence. It is said that a hundred guests sat down every night to dinner. As a patron he took an interest in his building at times embarrassing to his architect. It was either this fact that caused the incongruity of the enormous loggia facing the small garden; or the hope that in less troublous times the encircling wall would be removed and the loggia be the culmination to one of the main streets leading from the river. The wall rises at times to a gigantic height and, together with the aviary in one

corner, is decorated with seaweed and rock reminiscent of Genoa. The garden itself provides considerable interest for its small size, open and enclosed being contrasted. The star shape fills the angles ingeniously, and may possibly have been due to the astronomical feelings of the owner. Wallenstein was assassinated in the palace on 25 February, 1634.

Schönbrunn, the Gloriette

*Schönbrunn, the former menagerie,
now the Vienna Zoo*

*Schönbrunn, vista down clipped
hedges*

190

Schönbrunn, 'Roman' ruins

SCHWARZENBERG PALACE, VIENNA

(Built for Heinrich Mansfield, Count of Fondi. Begun 1697 possibly by J. Lukas von Hildebrandt, completed about 1715 by Fischer von Erlach. Sculpture by Lorenzo Mattei)

The engravings of Salomon Kleiner people the streets of Vienna with every kind of individual. The city was the centre of concourse of many nationalities, and the bright colours of army and retainers' uniforms mingled with the odd costumes of the populace itself. Coaches negotiated as best they could the narrow, twisting streets. Though the old houses were being rebuilt, space did not allow for road widening, and the fine Baroque palaces were designed to be seen in steep perspective. In contrast to this confusion and crush, the spaciousness of the Schwarzenberg Palace, with its cool garden and lavish forecourt opening towards the fortifications, was inviting. The building was started by Heinrich Mansfield, a rival of his neighbour Prince Eugene of Savoy, but he died before its completion and the palace came into the ownership of the present family.

Today the palace dominates the Schwarzenberg Platz, effacing the Belvedere palaces. From the relation of the three great estates, the Schwarzenberg, the Belvedere and the Salesian Nunnery, it seems that the jostling of buildings within the fortifications was echoed traditionally beyond the open girdle.

Bellotto's painting of the Schwarzenberg and Belvedere shows the contrast between the two gardens. The Belvedere is a view terrace, with a shady garden below. The Schwarzenberg is a shade garden with an open terrace above. Though one side has now been curtailed to widen the Prinz Eugen Strasse, and the gardens are not so well preserved as those of its neighbour, the place has aged with considerable charm. The sculpture is vigorous or languorous according to position. The chestnuts of the upper terraces have grown to an immense size and beneath them the lines of the old garden at times disappear. These tall trees conceal the theme of the garden: the climb from the palace through shade until the last ramp should lift the terrace above the hedges. There lay the view of Vienna.

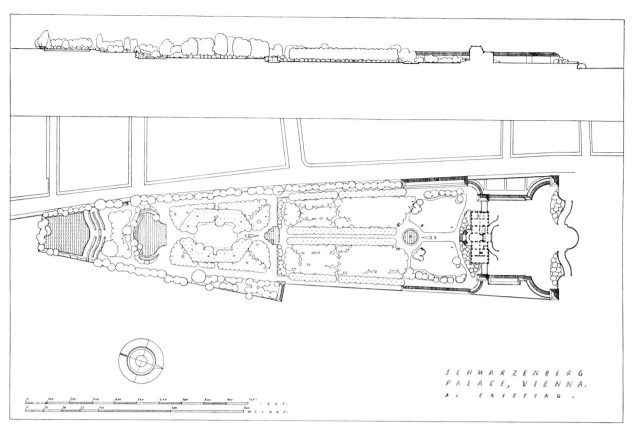

Plan and section as existing

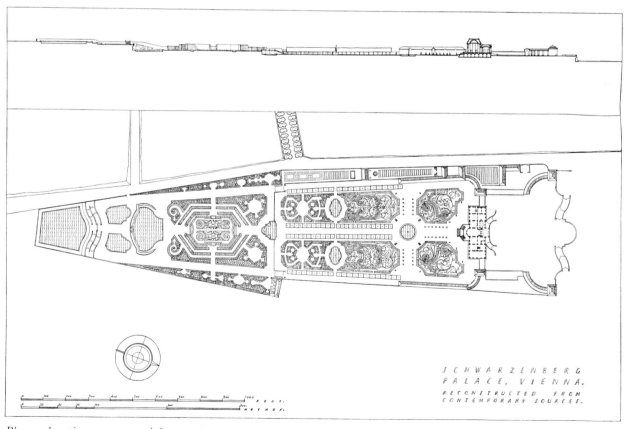

Plan and section reconstructed from contemporary sources

continued

Schwarzenberg palace from the painting by Bernardo Bellotto

Two views of Schwarzenberg palace grounds, Vienna

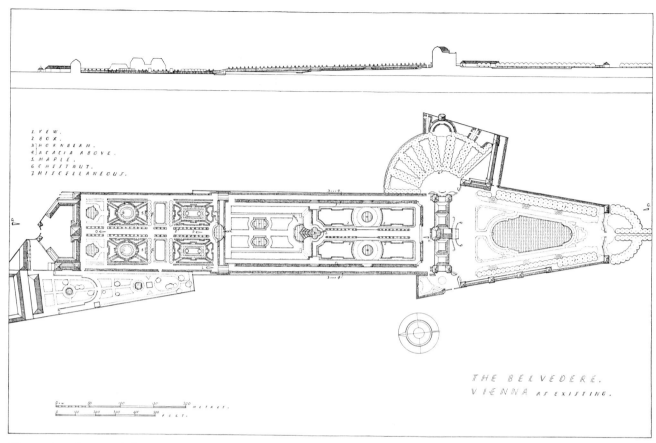

1. Y E W.
2. B O X.
3. H O R N B E A M.
4. A C A C I A   A B O V E.
5. M A P L E.
6. C H E S T N U T.
7. M I S C E L L A N E O U S.

THE BELVEDERE.
VIENNA AS EXISTING.

Plan and section as existing

THE BELVEDERE, VIENNA

(The lower palace completed 1716, the upper completed 1723, for Prince Eugene of Savoy. Architect Lukas von Hildebrandt. The gardens in collaboration with François Girard)

A set of engravings by Salomon Kleiner published in 1731 bore the following title: 'The Wonderful Home of the Incomparable Hero of our time in Wars and Victories; or the actual Presentation and Copy of Garden, Court, and Pleasure Buildings, belonging to his most Serene Highness, Prince Eugenius Franciscus, Duke of Savoy, etc.' The private life of Prince Eugene appears to have been held in equal esteem. Yet the Emperor was so surrounded by intrigue that at times the Prince was forced to retaliate to maintain his position. He out-manoeuvred his enemies, and dying in 1736 at the age of 72, left behind buildings that are a testimony to his greatness. Undeniably he enjoyed display, and when in 1693 Leopold provided the means for a palace and presented the strip of land beyond the Schwarzenberg, he determined to eclipse his rivals. The same year he took command in Hungary, and returning later in triumph found that the vineyards overlooking his land from the east had been sold to the Salesian Sisters.

The Lower Belvedere, with the immediate garden shade and Kammergarten, was the dwelling place. Here came the prince from his congested winter palace and lived in view of the building that epitomised his triumphs. Before the windows lay the clipped hedges, walls of maple twelve

continued

feet high and a foot thick. The centre features of fountains and cascades rose one above the other, glistening against the dark background of the upper palace. To the right through iron gates lay the Kammergarten, today marred by the placing of modern sculpture. To the left towered the blank wall of the nunnery, whose skyline the Prince might well dislike.

The upper palace was used for entertaining and receptions, and the garden as it extends towards this grows more open and less intimate. There are in fact two gardens, one for either palace, but the blending of the one into the other is scarcely perceptible. To one side lay the menagerie, for Prince Eugene was as fond of animals as of gardens (the idea of the plan was taken from that at Versailles); and the animals later formed the nucleus of the menagerie at Schönbrunn. On fête nights the great forecourt was lined with hundreds of waiting coaches. The approach was spectacular, for coaches after passing the entrance gates divided before the reflecting pool doubling the illuminations. It is said that at times as many as six thousand guests were present.

Colour plates pages 186 and 187

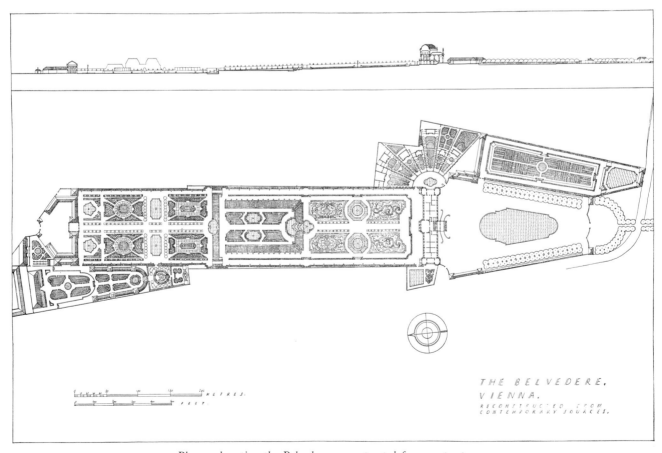

Plan and section the Belvedere, reconstructed from contemporary sources

Engravings of the Belvedere by Salomon Kleiner

continued

Six views of the Belvedere, Vienna

198

continued

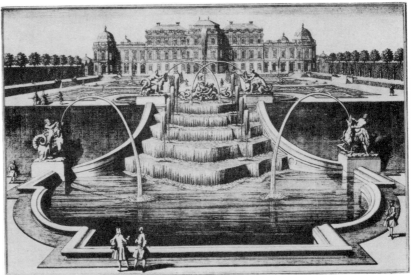

Engravings of the Belvedere by
Salomon Kleiner

200

Aerial view of the Belvedere, Vienna

continued

The Belvedere, Vienna

Plan reconstructed from an engraving by Salomon Kleiner

SCHLOSS SCHONBORN, GOLLERSDORF

(Built for Friedrich Karl von Schonborn by Lukas von Hildebrandt. Completed 1717)

Fischer von Erlach built the winter palace in Vienna for the Count of Schonborn as early as 1700. In the following years he was displaced as architect by Hildebrandt, who appears to have carried out considerable work for the branches of this extensive family. Having completed the summer palace beyond the fortifications he began another at Gollersdorf about thirty miles north-west of the city. The countryside is uninteresting. Though avenues run out on all sides, they do so for no purpose and the scheme suggests how small a part landscape plays in the Austrian garden. Palace, orangery, and most of the avenues exist today. All pools, fountains, parterres, and garden features have been altered or removed, and the park has been partially 'landscaped.' The fanciful shapes and converging rectangle shown on the original design were to counteract monotony given by a flat site. Palace and orangery are well related, but the defect of detail in certain parts is as flagrant as at the upper Belvedere, and must have detracted from an otherwise distinguished design.

continued

Schloss Schonborn, Gollersdorf

MIRABELL GARDENS, SALZBURG

(Built 1606 for Archbishop Wolf Dietrich. New garden begun 1689 for Johann Ernst Count Thun possibly by Fischer von Erlach. Palace remodelled 1721-7 by Lukas von Hildebrandt; partly rebuilt after a fire 1818. Garden theatre by B. Maindl)

Salzburg lies upon both banks of the Salzac between the steep Monchsberg and the Kapuzinerberg. All around are fertile plains spreading to the Alps. The quiet squares, fountains, and two horseponds bring into the old town huddling together a sense of freshness and repose. Within a few minutes' climb from any point are virgin woods. Many of the buildings have gardens, and in the Arenberg gasse a series climbs the abrupt Kapuzinerberg to overlook the town and Hohensalzburg. Here is carried the sound of the bells from the belfries, the carillon of the Neugebaude, and the horn from the castle; for Salzburg, the home of Mozart, was always a city of music.

In this setting are the Mirabell gardens. The palace was built outside the city by Wolf Dietrich for his beautiful Salome Alt, the cause of his downfall six years later. The following century the whole character was changed. Though the palace was again rebuilt in 1818, and the great forecourt has been absorbed by the town, the general disposition of the gardens now is that of the early eighteenth cnetury.

To a Baroque architect accustomed to deal with wider areas the lines of the ramparts must have been restraining. The compromise of filling the space allotted, however, brought the scale of the gardens unconsciously into relation with that of the town. The principal axis lies along the row of clipped trees. This should be terminated by the building shown in the engraving (overleaf), to complete the design, and is flanked by the main garden laid out on the view of Hohensalzburg. The four main groups of sculpture are probably the most remarkable of their kind in Austria or Germany, and are partially reflected in the smaller vases and balustrading.

Perhaps much of the charm of the Mirabell gardens lies in the odd unexpected corners. Across a bridge there is an island given up to stone dwarfs that were a fashion of the period and represent the best and most hideous of their kind. The aviary with its little garden is now overcrowded, but the erection itself has some of the grace of the later and more ambitious example at Schönbrunn. Upon a rampart, and now approached through the trellis walk, is a garden theatre of hornbeam, cunningly planned for the space it fills.

continued

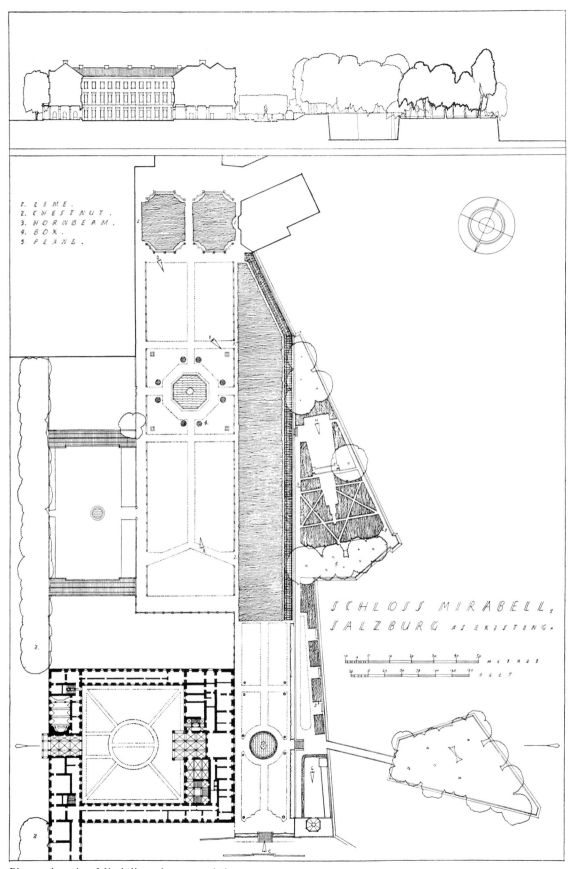

1. LIME.
2. CHESTNUT.
3. HORNBEAM.
4. BOX.
5. PLANE.

SCHLOSS MIRABELL,
SALZBURG AS EXISTING.

Plan and section Mirabell gardens, as existing

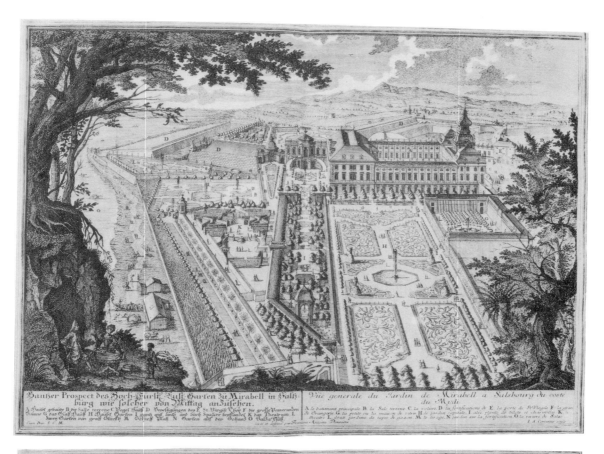

Engravings of the Mirabell gardens by R.A. Danreiter, 1760

continued

Six views of the Mirabell gardens, Salzburg

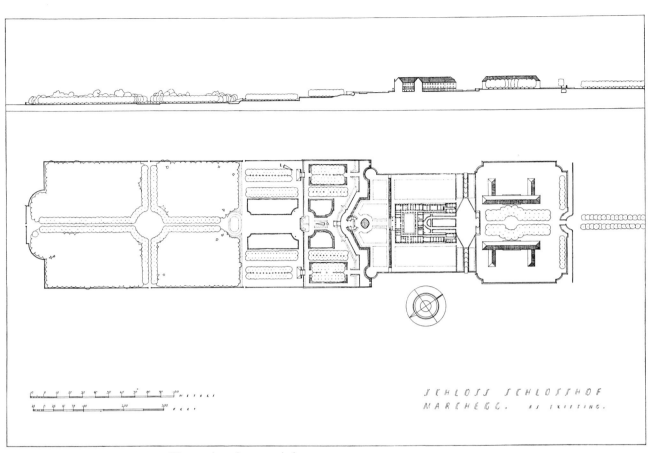

Plan and section as existing

SCHLOSS SCHLOSSHOF, MARCHEGG

(Acquired and rebuilt by Prince Eugene of Savoy, 1725. Altered 1755 by Maria Theresa. Architect for palace, Fischer von Erlach, for gardens possibly Lukas von Hildebrandt)

The imperial palace of Schlosshof lies on rising ground thirty miles east of Vienna, facing views to the east. As an old semi-fortified manor it was acquired by Prince Eugene, who enlarged the building and began the magnificent garden. Later it was owned and considerably altered by Maria Theresa, Bellotto's pictures being painted here soon after 1758. Now it is almost derelict. The graceful touches have gone, and the stark buildings remain; ironwork and much of the sculpture were only recently removed, and a straight ramp has replaced the curved approach. Throughout the garden the terraces, fragments of sculpture, and overgrown trees, are a faint echo of its past grandeur, for after Schönbrunn Schlosshof was perhaps the most ambitious garden in Austria. It was sufficiently far from the capital to be free of immediate contact, and not too far for the splendid fêtes that were occasionally held.

The ramparts round the house and stables are above the surrounding level, and it was to these that the new gardens were attached. The circular stairs are

Schloss Schlosshof from paintings by Bernardo Bellotto

ingeniously carved out the centre bastion, but this does not conceal a junction most apparent where the side walls abut the corner bastions. Seen from below the terraces lead up dramatically to the palace. The addition of a top floor made the building itself too high and added to the sense of isolation of palace from garden. This is more noticeable in the paintings even before the addition than it is today, for trees have grown up to break the skyline.

The only suggestive difference between this plan and that of a town garden is the hint of ramps in the latter. The gardeners with their barrows and rollers mingling with the courtiers were as much a matter of everyday life as the curious contrasts in the streets themselves. The absence of ramps at Schlosshof (for the side lanes were used), and the consequent lack of association is a clue to the character. One gigantic terrace is separated too abruptly from another. The design shows complete mastery over garden technique: shady walks, spectacular effects, variety, and good quality of detail. It appears immature mainly because the modelling is unconvincing.

continued

Schloss Schlosshof from the painting by Bernardo Bellotto

Two views of Schloss Schlosshof, Marchegg

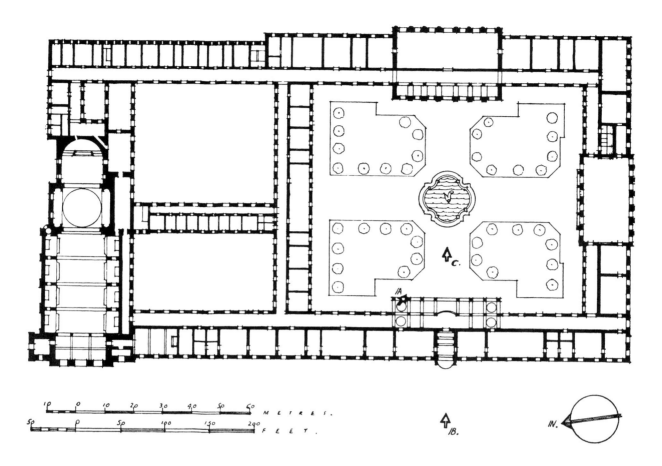

Plan of first floor as existing

ABBEY OF ST. FLORIAN

(Augustinian abbey since 1071. Rebuilding begun 1686 by Carlantonio Carlone, completed by Jakob Prandauer 1751. Fountain in court by Sattler)

St. Florian is one of the series of monasteries that lie within reach of the Danube between Vienna and Linz. The situation is not comparable to that of Melk or Gottweig, but architecturally it is equally gorgeous. These vast self-contained units are all remarkable for their general use of composition and exuberant detail. The detail when analysed is usually gross, but the disposition and treatment shows the genius of the stage. The centre court at St. Florian, approached through Carlone's doorway, is perhaps the most sumptuous of that of any monastery in Austria. The simplicity of the planting is a foil to the fountain, the great open stair, and the façades around. The whole well-balanced group is arranged independent of gardens about the exterior. These are commonplace and haphazard, though something of the effort necessary to put the buildings on their platform is suggested by the huge retaining walls to the west and north.

continued

Abbey of St. Florian

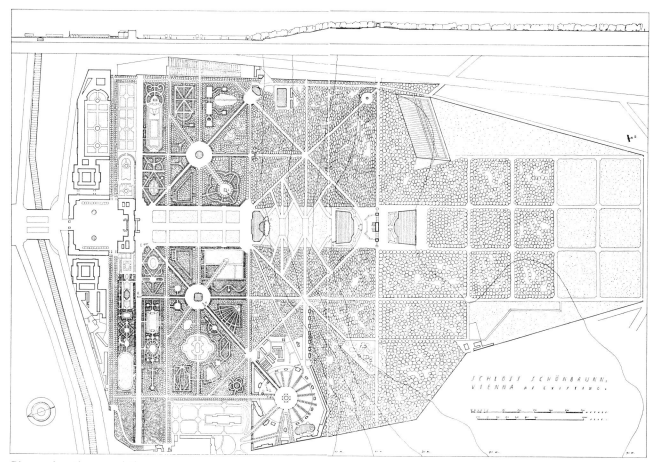

Plan and section as existing

SCHONBRUNN, VIENNA

(Hunting box destroyed by Turks, 1683. Plans prepared 1693 for Leopold I by Fischer von Erlach. Building continued 1744 for Maria Theresa by Picassi. Park designed by Fischer von Erlach, Adrian Steckhoven, von Hohenburg, and others. Gloriette (1775), obelisk, ruins (1778), etc., by von Hohenburg. Menagerie added 1752. Sculpture by Beyer, Hagenauer, Platzer and others)

From the earliest times the Habsburgs were keen hunters, and Maximilian II was probably the first to have a hunting box at Schönbrunn. His son Matthias gave the name 'Beautiful Spring.' Whatever may have been the shape of the earlier park, it is certain there existed long avenues cut through the forest. The bright array of hunters crossed and recrossed the vistas and the sound of the horn echoed from end to end. This tradition resisted Italian, French, and Dutch influences, and, later, that of England. Accessibility to Vienna, within fifteen minutes' drive, gave the palace a relation to the capital similar, in a smaller way, to that which Versailles has to Paris. Although successive Habsburgs in turn favoured other residences, Schönbrunn is the only one that can be described as the country seat of the dynasty. The present form dates from the time of Maria Theresa, whose personality more than that of anyone else is everywhere.

continued

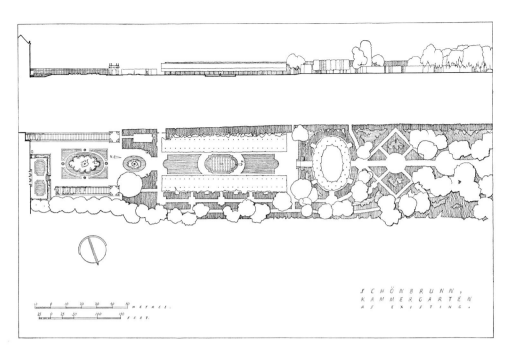

Plan and section
Kammergarten, Schönbrunn

After the forecourt and the way under the palace the first impression of the park is overwhelming. There is a vast rectangle. This space leads away to the foot of the hill, pauses on a flamboyant group of sculpture, and ascends to the airy building on the summit. On either side tower walls of hedge through which avenues are cut and disappear diagonally. By the side of the palace is the Kammergarten, separated from the great cross walk by a dainty trellis.

Within the blocks of hedges are hosts of things. On the east there is the aviary, one of the most fanciful of garden creations. At the foot of the hill astride an avenue, are sham Roman ruins, built possibly at the suggestion of Winckelmann; the publication of engravings by Piranesi in 1753 had drawn the attention of all Europe to ancient Rome. Past the obelisk and farther up the hill is the Little Gloriette, and an avenue leads hence along the brow to the Gloriette itself. From this position the entire park is seen. The bright parterre is peopled with moving specks framed between the warm yellow of the palace of Bellotto's painting, and the dark green hedges. Away beyond the palace the modern suburbs of Vienna cover the slopes leading up to the Wiener Wald; the city itself is well to the east. Down the steep zig-zag paths and once more through bosquets and clipped walks, it is a few minutes to the menagerie. This has been enlarged and is now the Vienna Zoo, but refreshment and gossip once took place in the centre pavilion, whence radiate the cages. To one side the hot-houses, initiated by Steckhoven, suggest the Dutch enthusiasm for horticulture; expeditions for rare plants were sent as far afield as South America and the West Indies.

After the death of Maria Theresa, Schönbrunn continued to be the royal palace, and the gardens are crowded with less happy memories. The unfortunate Duke of Reichstadt, 'Napoleon II,' died in the palace a prisoner of Metternich. Francis Joseph lived and died in the rooms overlooking the Kammergarten. The same building that had seen the rise of the Habsburg dynasty as a power in Europe saw the fall, for here the Emperor Charles signed his abdication in 1918.

Colour plates pages 190 and 191

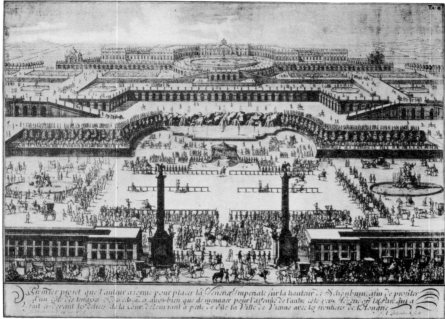

Two views of Schönbrunn from paintings by Bernardo Bellotto

Schönbrunn, first design by Fischer von Erlach

continued

Schönbrunn, aerial view

The palace of Schönbrunn

Schönbrunn, the Gloriette

Schönbrunn, the Gloriette

View in the grounds of Schönbrunn

continued

Six views of Schönbrunn

continued

Three views of Schönbrunn

BIBLIOGRAPHY

The following is a selection of the works consulted:

Baedeker, *Austria,* 1929.

Blomfield, Sir Reginald, *Byways,* 1929.

Coxe, W., *History of the House of Austria,* 1807.

Danreiter, F.A., *Lust-Stuck der Garten,* 1750; *Prospect von Hellbrunn,* 1760.

Delsenbach, J.A., *Vorstellungen der Vornehmsten Gebaude von Wien,* 1730.

Fischer, Johann Bernard, *Entwurff einer historischen Architektur,* 1721.

Furtenbach, Joseph, *Architectura Civilis,* 1628.

Gedye, G.E.R., *A Wayfarer in Austria,* 1928.

Gothein, M.L., *A History of Garden Art,* 1928.

Grimschitz, Bruno, *Joh. Lukas von Hildebrandt,* 1922; *Das Wiener Belvedere,* 1921.

Haller, Max, *Geschichte von Schlosshof.*

Ilg, Albert, *Prince Eugene of Savoy,* 1889; *Fischer von Erlach,* 1895.

Kleiner, Salomon, *Delineatio Omnium Templorum,* Wien, 1724; *Residences Memorables de Eugène François etc.,* 1731; *Menagerie de Eugène de Savoye,* 1734.

Lanchester, H.V., *Fischer von Erlach,* 1924.

Leisching, Julius, Paper on Salzburg gardens, Salzburg, 1926.

Levetus, A.S., *Imperial Vienna,* 1905.

Merian the Elder, Engravings, 1642.

Osterreichische Kunst-Topographie, Vols. I to 16, 1907 et seq.

Osterreichische Kunstbucher, published by Ed. Holzel. 1920 et seq.

Salaburg, Baroness Barbara von, *Engravings of Upper Austria,* 1640.

Schuetz, Carl, *Views of Vienna,* 1779.

Sedlmayr, Hans, *Osterreichische Barockarchitektur,* 1930.

Sitwell, Sacheverell, *German Baroque Art.*

Tietze, Hans, *Die Bildhauerie der Barockzeit,* 1927.

Triggs, F. Inigo, *Garden Craft in Europe,* 1913.

Whitman, Sidney, 'Austria,' Story of the Nations series, 1885.

INDEX

Page numbers in italics indicate illustrations